Top 25 locator map
◄

TwinPack
Sardinia

ADELE EVANS

Adele Evans is a travel writer and occasional broadcaster with a special interest in and love of Italy. She has written and contributed to many travel books as well as newspaper, magazine and online publications. She first sampled Sardinian *dolce vita* in the 1980s and returns to the island as often as possible. When she is not travelling, she lives in the New Forest, England.

If you have any comments or suggestions for this guide you can contact the editor at *Twinpacks@theAA.com*

AA Publishing
Find out more about AA Publishing and the wide range of travel publications and services the AA provides by visiting our website at *www.theAA.com/travel*

Contents

About this book

TwinPack Sardinia is divided into six sections to cover the six most important aspects of your visit to the island. It includes:

- The author's view of Sardinia and its people
- Suggested walks and drives
- The Top 25 sights to visit
- The best of the rest – aspects of Sardinia that make it special
- Detailed listings of restaurants, hotels, shops and nightlife
- Practical information

In addition, easy-to-read side panels provide fascinating extra facts and snippets, highlights of places to visit and invaluable practical advice.

CROSS-REFERENCES

To help you make the most of your visit, cross-references, indicated by ▶, show you where to find additional information about a place or subject.

MAPS

The fold-out map in the wallet at the back of the book is a large-scale map of Sardinia.

The Top 25 locator maps found on the inside front cover and inside back cover of the book itself are for quick reference. They show the Top 25 Sights, described on pages 24–48, which are clearly plotted by number (**1**–**25**, not page number) in alphabetical order.

PRICES

Where appropriate, an indication of the cost of an attraction is given by ✋ Expensive, Moderate or Inexpensive. An indication of the cost of a restaurant is given by € signs: €€€ denotes higher prices, €€ denotes average prices, while € denotes lower prices.

SARDINIA
life

A Personal View

Cast away in the middle of the Mediterranean, Sardinia is often nicknamed 'the small continent'. It has idyllic ivory beaches lapped by silky waters in every shade of turquoise blue. Venture inland and you will find a traditional land of shepherds, of wild landscape sprinkled with prehistoric sites, rolling hills and meadows bright with wild flowers. It is extraordinary to think that an island right in the heart of Europe can be so beautiful and so unspoilt.

Sardinia is the second-largest island in the Mediterranean after Sicily. It belongs to Italy and is equidistant from Italy and the coast of Tunisia, lying 200km from both. The writer D. H. Lawrence described it as being 'lost between Europe and Africa and belonging to nowhere'. And he went on to say, 'It gives a sense of space. It is like liberty itself.'

The rolling countryside around Santa Trinità di Saccargia

Go inland and you will be amazed, too, by the liberating peace of the wild and empty interior, broken only by the tinkling bells of sheep and goats. In little villages people will stare incredulously as if they have never seen a car before. On hillocks, scented with the deliciously pungent *macchia*, circular stone ruins rise up – unique prehistoric rock villages, of which 7,000 remain, built by the Nuraghic civilization. The tombs of the Nuraghic tribal chiefs were known as 'giants' tombs' (*tombe dei giganti*), while the 'fairy houses' (*domus de janas*), carved into the hillside and rock faces, pre-date them, going back into the mists of time.

And then there is, of course, the coast and the fabled Costa Smeralda – home of the glitterati. In the 1950s, while yachting in the northeast of the island, the fabulously wealthy Prince Karim Aga Khan IV and his chums became spellbound by the translucent emerald-green waters and romantic little coves. And so was born the Costa Smeralda in the 1960s. Those jewel colours take on every hue from sapphire blue to sparkling

The blue-green waters of the Bàia Sardinia, on the northeast coast

WILD HERBS

Macchia mediterranea (Mediterranean maquis) is a highly scented, tangled array of lavender, rosemary, wild fennel, herbs, and plants such as juniper, myrtle and strawberry tree. Plants unknown to the mainland thrive here and the phrase 'sardonic grin' comes from the grimace found on victims poisoned by a certain herb found in Sardinia that contains strychnine-like alkaloids.

turquoise, so dazzling in contrast with the sugar-white sands that you can't help but sport your designer shades.

Great swathes of the Sardinian coast remain uninhabited, with pines, juniper and prickly pears encircling occasional sandy beaches, sea and granite rocks. The coastline of almost 2,000km is indented by tiny coves, picturesque harbours and rugged cliffs. It is a quarter of the total Italian coast and has Italy's best beaches. Yet for the Sardinians the sea was traditionally synonymous with those who came to plunder – '*furat chi beit dae su mare*' ('he who comes from the sea comes to rob'). Phoenicians, Romans, Arabs, Catalans and mainland Italians have all left their mark, but those unique prehistoric stones towers, *nuraghi*, bear testament to the Sardinians' long history of independence. And taking this independent trait into modern times, the president of Sardinia, Renato Soru, elected in 2004, made it his task to protect the coastline from the ravages of developers and to uphold the traditions of the islanders.

No other folkloric tradition in Europe survives so completely as in Sardinia. Fabulous festivals, gusty flavours and feasting and not a little magic interwoven with stories of fairies and giants are all part of the intoxicating Sard charm.

Whether it's the gorgeous spring and autumn flowers, the wind-sculpted granite rocks, the rare birds and wildlife already extinct on the mainland or the sybaritic charms of sand and sea, this extraordinarily varied place is an island for all seasons – truly, a 'small continent'.

Wildflowers carpet the island

Sardinia in Figures

GEOGRAPHY

- Sardinia is in the Mediterranean, lying 200km north of the African coast and the same distance west of mainland Italy.
- It has an area of 24,090sq km, and is the second largest island in the Mediterranean after Sicily.
- The highest point is Punta La Mármora in the Gennargentu, at 1,834m.
- The island is 350km long from north to south.
- The coastline is 1,849km long.
- The population is 1.65 million, of which about 163,000 live in Cágliari.

CLIMATE

- Sardinia is usually hot and dry for a six-month summer from May to October.
- The mildest months on the coast are May and October.
- The *maestrale* (mistral) wind from the north-west sweeps the island, and the hot scirocco from the south often brings sand.
- Winters are generally cold and rainy, with snow in the mountainous interior, but may be mild on the coast.
- April is generally cool and unpredictable.

ECONOMIC FACTORS

- Sardinia is an autonomous region – one of five in Italy entitled to administer themselves.
- The island's economy is traditionally based on tourism, farming and fishing. President Renato Soru has swung the  focus more on industry, commerce, services and information technology. The island is also becoming known for its excellent wines.

  Market-fresh fish, Sássari

- Vast tracts of cork oak make Sardinia Italy's largest supplier of cork.
- There are almost 4 million sheep on Sardinia – more than a third of Italy's total.
- The unemployment rate is 20 per cent.

People of Sardinia

Grazia Deledda

Born in Núoro in 1871, Grazia Deledda was one of Italy's most important early 20th-century realist writers and the first Italian woman to win the Nobel Prize for Literature (1926). Her writings portray life on her native island with depth and sympathy and deal with human problems in general, and are by no means romantic portrayals of Sardinian small-town and rural life. She lived in Núoro for 29 years, and her birthplace museum gives an insight into life in a Nuorese house, together with her memorabilia, including first editions of her books, press clippings and her old photos. Her most famous book, *Canne al Vento* (*Reeds in the Wind*), contains the well-known line 'We are reeds and fate is the wind.' She died in 1936 and is buried at the foot of Monte Ortobene in the church of Santa Maria della Solitudine.

Giuseppe Garibaldi

Often likened to an Italian Che Guevara, the revolutionary Giuseppe Garibaldi (1807–82) made the island of Caprera his home in 1855. It was his refuge after his campaigns in the pursuit of Italian unification and he found solace in the peace and wild nature of this island. He was a great crusader and warrior, who commanded the 'volunteers' and conquered most of the country. He tried to reassure the Sardinians of their common destiny, writing: 'Sardinia is the most important and strategically most significant place in the Mediterranean.'

Renato Soru

Born in 1957 in Sanluri, billionaire Renato Soru (founder of internet service provider Tiscali) was elected president of Sardinia in 2004. He made the preservation of the island's environment a personal crusade, freezing all building within 3km of the coast and levying a luxury tax on non-resident owners of luxury villas, super yachts and private planes. 'The island's Wild West period is over,' he said. At the same time he has sought to restore vitality to the interior. 'Now a different model of development is possible,' he added, 'one based on the culture of the local people.'

Giuseppe Garibaldi, hero of the Italian unification (Risorgimento)

A Chronology

350000BC	Early Palaeolithic settlers' flint tools found.
13000BC	Cave-dwellers' bones found dating to end of Late Palaeolithic age.
6000BC	Obsidian tools are traded with Corsica and France.
4000–2700BC	*Domus de janas* tombs ('fairy houses') are evidence of the Ozieri culture.
1600–900BC	Era of the *nuraghi* – cone-shaped stone citadels and megalithic *tombe dei giganti* (giants' tombs).
900–232BC	Phoenicians, then Carthaginians, establish trading posts in Sardinia (Cágliari, Thárros, Sant'Antíoco, Nora and Ólbia).
241BC–AD400	Roman occupation of Sardinia.
AD456	Barbarian tribe, the Vandals, arrive.
534–10th century	Byzantine rule. Sardinia becomes one of Byzantium's seven African provinces.
1015–1297	Pisans and Genoese help Sardinia defeat an Arab fleet from Mallorca and the island comes under Pisan, then Genoese, control.
1297	Spanish kingdom of Aragon creates kingdom of Sardinia and Corsica and Sardinia remains under Spanish rule for the next three centuries.
15th century	Famine and plague reduce Sardinia's population from 340,000 to 150,000.
1708	During the Spanish War of Succession, English and Austrian forces seize Sardinia from King Philip V of Spain.
1720	The Duke of Savoy, Vittorio Amedeo II, becomes the King of Piedmont and Sardinia.
1735–38	The Viceroy De Rivarolo tries but fails to rid the island of *banditismo* – clan warfare, robbery and kidnapping.

1797–99	Army of the French Republic invades Italy and King Charles III of Piedmont takes refuge in Sardinia.
1804–05	Admiral Horatio Nelson is based on Sardinia for 15 months. He recognises the island's strategic importance, calling it 'the finest island in the Mediterranean'.
1823	Enclosures Act, defining pastoral and agricultural land and abolition of communal rights, results in riots. Banditry becomes rife again.
1847	Sardinia and Piedmont form an alliance, but Sardinia pays a heavy price for the unification of Italy.
1861	Vittorio Emanuele II of Piedmont becomes king of Italy; Sardinia is no longer a kingdom.
1870–1900	Nomadic sheep-farming on the increase as well as banditry. Miners' strikes reach a climax at Buggerru in 1904.
1915	Italy enters World War I on the Allied side and 13,000 Sardinians die on the battlefield. The bravery of the Brigata Sassari changes the way the mainland Italians view Sardinia.
1940–48	Italy enters World War II on the German side. Three-quarters of Cágliari is destroyed in Allied bombing raids. Sardinia becomes an autonomous region.
1962	The Aga Khan creates the fashionable Costa Smeralda resort.
1985	Francesco Cossiga from Sássari becomes president of the Italian Republic.
2004	Multimedia billionaire Renato Soru (born 1957) is elected president of Sardinia and imposes controversial new 'luxury taxes'.
2007	Italian government files suit against 'luxury taxes' in constitutional court.

Best of Sardinia

Louis Vuitton shop on the Piazzetta, Porto Cervo

If you have only a short time to visit Sardinia, or would like to get a complete picture of the island, here are the essentials:

- There are beautiful beaches all along the coastline; sample as many as you can.
- In the northwest, the Spiaggia della Pelosa, Stintino, is a must-see for its adjective-defying blue waters.
- In the northeast, head for the Costa Smeralda beaches such as Cala Liscia Ruia and Spiaggia Capriccioli, which are well known and have easy access. Others, such as the exquisite Portu Li Coggi (or Spiaggia del Principe, Prince's Beach), have more difficult access but reward with their beauty.
- On the east coast, around the Golfo di Orosei, take your pick of gorgeous beaches such as Cala Luna and the spectacular grottos, such as the Grotta del Bue Marino.
- In the south, be dazzled by the talcum-powder white beaches around Báia Chia.
- Head off the beaten track for the Arcipélago de La Maddalena, with its castaway islands and *macchia*-scented vegetation on Ísola Caprera.
- Trek through the rugged and spectacular scenery in Tiscali and Gorruppu Gorge.
- The island is sprinkled with fascinating archaeological sites. If you visit only one, the Nuraghe Su Nuraxi is *the nuraghe*.
- Marvel at the *domus de janas* (fairy houses) and *tombe dei giganti* (giants' tombs) around Arzachena.
- Drive from Alghero to Bosa or from Cágliari to Villasimíus for amazing coastal scenery.
- See some of the best wild scenery around the Gennargentu and Golfo di Orosei. And drink in the views from Monte Ortobene.
- Take an evening stroll along the sea walls of Alghero, dotted with bars and restaurants.
- Walk around the Castello area of the capital, Cágliari, by the Bastione San Remy and enjoy the views and buzzing nightlife.
- Rub shoulders with the glitterati at Porto Cervo's Piazzetta.

Rocky path through Gola Su Gorruppu gorge

SARDINIA
how to organise your time

13

A Walk around Cágliari

INFORMATION

Distance 4km
Time 3–4 hours
Start point Bastione San Remy
End point Via Roma
Lunch Caffè degli Spiriti (€)
✉ Bastione San Remy

This route takes you through the Castello, the historic heart of Cágliari, down to the bustling Via Roma, overlooking the waterfront.

Start from Bastione San Remy, Piazza Costituzione. Heading north, walk up the Via Fossario to Piazza Palazzo, the heart of the Castello district and to the Cattedrale on your right. Admire the Pisan Romanesque façade and the baroque/Gothic interior.

Continue northwards and turn right into the little Piazzetta Mercede Mundula and admire the glorious views over the Bay of Cágliari. Continue up the Via Pietro Martini to the Piazza Indipendenza. At the head of this piazza is the medieval Torre di San Pancrazio, a symbol of Cágliari. Go through the archway to the Piazza Arsenale to the Cittadella dei Musei.

Of the four museums here, the Museo Archeológico Nazionale (▶ 58) is the highlight. It gives a fascinating insight into Sardinia's past and is the island's best archaeological museum.

On leaving the museum turn right and go out of Porta Cristina. Turn right along Viale Buon Cammino then cross over the road with Via Anfiteatro on your left and continue along Viale Buon Cammino with the Anfiteatro Romano on your left. Turn left at the next junction down Via Frà Ignazio da Laconi and arrive at the entrance to the 2nd century AD Roman amphitheatre.

View over the city through Bastione San Remy's archway

Keep following the road down and turn left, still in Via Fra Ignazio da Laconi till you arrive at Ingresso No 11 for the Orto Botánico. These botanic gardens are a pleasant shady spot.

On exit, turn left into Via Portoscalas past Chiesa di San Michele. Turn right into Corso Vittorio Emanuele II, then right into Largo Carlo Felice and straight down to the Via Roma.

A Walk around Alghero

This walk takes you through the old town of Alghero, protected by ancient walls and towers with washing hung out like bunting.

Start at Piazza Porta Terra, opposite the top end of the Giardino Púbblico, and drop into the Porta Terra, which was one of the walled town's two gates, and is now an interpretation centre. From the top there are excellent views. From here turn left into Carrer de los Arjoles, then right into Via Ambrogion Machin. At the end of this road, turn right into Via Carlo Alberto and continue on to the Chiesa di San Francesco on the right, one of Alghero's landmarks with its stately, pointed Aragonese tower.

From the church turn left and walk back down Via Carlo Alberto. This street is Alghero's main shopping hub, full of boutiques and jewellery shops brimming with coral. Continue straight on crossing over Via Gilbert Ferret and on the left you come to the 17th-century Chiesa di San Michele with its glistening ceramic dome.

Walk back to Via Gilbert Ferret and turn left then right into Via Principe Umberto, one of the old centre's most attractive lanes. On your left is the Jamaica Inn. Continue up the Via Principe Umberto till you come to the cathedral's octagonal campanile. Walk around into Piazza Duomo.

Walk east past Via Maiorca, Via Carlo Alberto and Vicolo Sena till you arrive at Piazza Cívica, the old town's main square, known as '*Il Salotto*' (the dining room). It is just inside the Porta Mare (Sea Gate) and is full of alfresco bars.

INFORMATION

Distance 2km
Time 2–3 hours
Start point Piazza Porta Terra
End point Piazza Cívica
Lunch Il Ghiotto (€)
    ✉ Piazza Cívica 23
    ☎ 079 974820

Dining alfresco in Piazza Cívica, with the Palazzo d'Albis behind

15

A Walk on the Island of Goats

This walk takes you through the *macchia* and green pines on the island of Caprera, 'Garibaldi's island' (▶ 32), with magnificent views over the Arcipélago de La Maddalena (▶ 25).

Take the footpath that forks right into the *macchia* going south. After about 15 minutes, you reach a grove of umbrella pine trees. Continue, then turn right at the next fork and on your right is the Golfo di Stagnali beach.

Keep straight on the main track leading to an asphalt road on which you bear right. At the fork turn left and begin the ascent looking out over the archipelago's islands and Corsica. After about 1 hour 15 minutes you'll see the peak of Poggio Rasu (Bare Hill). The road bends to the left; carry along here, turning right and climbing upwards before the road begins to level out and descend. At a T-junction turn right past a derelict fountain on the left.

Continue along this road to a lay-by on the left (about 1 hour 50 minutes), then after 50m fork sharp right and climb up the steps to Monte Teialone (212m) – Caprera's highest peak, with a lookout tower.

Return to the road and turn right past a derelict house on the left. Follow the road left and, at a track junction, turn down to the left. Ignore the two turns on your right, going straight ahead. At a junction go left past two Military Zone buildings on the right and up to a reservoir (about 3 hours 15 minutes). Follow the ascending path which then flattens out leading to a car park. Take the granite drive on the right to the Museo Garibaldino (about 15 minutes).

Before the Garibaldi buildings, take the short concrete drive on the left to a little terrace. Carry on downhill on the path below the enclosed estate till the path descends between rocks. At a small house bear right before joining a road which takes you past more houses. Keep left on the main road and you will arrive back at the car park.

INFORMATION

Distance 12.5km
Time 7 hours
Start/end point Car park, Caprera (350m after causeway from La Maddalena)
Lunch Bring your own picnic, and plenty of water

Pause to admire the views from the island

A Drive from Cágliari to Villasimíus

This drive takes you past the Golfo degli Ángeli (Bay of Angels) along the Strada Panoramica, which overlooks lovely beaches backed by low hills covered with Mediterranean *macchia*.

From the centre of Cágliari, head for the waterfront and take the coastal road east, signposted Poetto and Villasimíus in the middle and outside lanes. You will pass many bars, cafés and restaurants – and plenty of joggers. Stop at the huge Poetto beach (➤ 52–53) with its fine, white sand, and/or admire the lagoon of Molentargius behind it, which is frequented by flamingos and many other species of wetland birdlife.

Continue on the coast road, following the local signs for Flúmini, in the direction of Villasimíus. The road now starts twisting and turning into a very scenic drive. About 21.5km from Cágliari you come to Torre delle Stelle. Take the dirt road east from the centre of the village, just east of the small passage above the villas crossed by the main road. Head east towards the coast until you reach the beach, where there are bars and shops by the white-golden sand. Retrace your steps to the main coastal road.

About 32km from Cágliari you will pick up signs for Solánas. The main road rings round giving access to the beach (Spiaggia Solánas). The large, golden sandy beach extends to the west of this promontory, overseen by a 16th-century watchtower, Torre di Capo Boi. Continue back on the main road and after 11km take the road to the right going south, signposted Capo Carbonara (2.5km). This is the most southeasterly point of Sardinia and from here there are excellent views. Rejoin the main road, which then brings you into Villasimíus (➤ 48).

INFORMATION

Distance 51 km (plus detours to beaches)
Time 2–3 hours, or full day with detours
Start point Cágliari
End point Villasimíus
Lunch Café del Porto (€–€€)
✉ Porto di Villasimíus

Rocky coastline between Cágliari and Villasimíus

17

A Drive down the Sínis Peninsula

This drive takes you past lagoons to the ancient Phoenician/Roman city of Thárros on the Sínis Peninsula and 'spaghetti western' country.

INFORMATION

Distance 49km
Time Half a day
Start/end point Oristano
Lunch Choice of cafés at Marina di Torre Grande on esplanade (€–€€€)

Take the SS292 north from Oristano towards Marina di Torre Grande and Cúglieri. Take the left fork following the signs for Cábras/Thárros and continue, following signs for San Giovanni di Sínis. Some 9km from Oristano you come to the buzzing seaside resort of Marina di Torre Grande. This is both Cábras's and Oristano's main beach and the palm-lined esplanade is full of bars and restaurants.

Head back to the main road and at the T-junction take the left-hand turn towards San Giovanni di Sínis. On both sides you now have lagoons – flamingo heaven. Go straight on, then take the right turn towards Thárros and continue down to the car park for which you pay €2 for two hours.

An old watchtower stands sentinel on the headland and the coast is fringed by lovely beaches, including the nearby beach of San Giovanni di Sínis.

After visiting Thárros (➤ 45), return the same way until you reach the signposted left turn to San Salvatore/Riola, 4km north. Once the setting for spaghetti westerns, the dusty little town of San Salvatore is hugely atmospheric. Stop at the San Salvatore 'wild west saloon', the only pub in the hamlet.

Go northeast on SP7 towards SP59 for 7km then turn right at the SS292 after 1km and take the next right at Via Sant'Anna into Riola Sardo (15.5km from San Salvatore to Riola Sardo). From here continue on the SS292 back to Oristano (12km from Riola Sardo).

Corinthian columns at Thárros

A Drive through the Gennargentu

This scenic drive takes you through granite-strewn, rolling, mountainous countryside framed by lush vegetation of *macchia*, cork, holm and oak trees.

Leave Núoro heading east on the Via Trieste. After 0.3km bear slight right onto the SP42, Via Monte Ortobene. Continue along this panoramic road as it twists upwards to the top of the mountain (8km from Núoro). Leave your car in the car park. A 100m walk along a dusty track, followed by a climb up 49 rock steps, will take you to the sculpture of Christ the Redeemer on top of Monte Ortobene.

Drive to Oliena (12km further on), heading northwest on the SP42 towards the SP45/Via Valverde. Bear slightly left at SP45/Viale La Solitudine and turn left at SP45. Take a sharp left at the SS129. After 4km, turn right at the SP22 and continue on the SP22 by turning left. Oliena is a very pretty town of white-washed old houses and its vineyards produce excellent wines. A little diversion 6km east on the Dorgali road/SP46 leads to Su Gologone, named after its spring. Return on the SP46 to Oliena. About 7km after Oliena turn left at the SP58 and follow this twisting, scenic road for about 11km until you see the entrance to Orgosolo, with a rock with a face painted on it, at the side of the road. Known as the 'capital of the Barbágia', it is also famous for its murals (► 55–56).

From Orgosolo head west for 10km to Mamoiada on the SP22. Famous for its masked festivals, especially at Carnival time, it has the interesting Museo delle Maschere Mediterannee showing the town's distinctive *mamuthones* costumed figures.

From Mamoiada, head southwest on Via Matteotti towards Via Núoro and turn right then bear slightly right again at SS389/Via Vittorio Emanuele II and follow the SS389 to Núoro (16.6km).

INFORMATION

Distance 77km
Time Half a day
Start/end point Núoro
Lunch Su Gologone Hotel's restaurant (€€€)
✉ Località Su Gologone
☎ 0784 287512

The winding road up Monte Ortobene

19

Finding Peace & Quiet

WALKING

The hills behind Alghero in the northwest, where only the tinkling bells of the sheep and goats disturb the peace, are perfect for walking. Around Santa Teresa and the Costa Smeralda coast there are glorious coastal paths from where you can admire the extraordinary granite rock formations sculpted by the wind and sea and, inland, the lunar landscape of the Valle della Luna. For more strenuous walking and trekking, the Gennargentu and Sopramonte mountain ranges in the east reward with spectacular views. Tucked away inside Monte Tiscali are the remains of a Nuraghic village, while, nearby, the spectacular Gola Su Gorruppu is one of Europe's deepest accessible canyons. Easily accessible from Cala Golone, the Golfo di Orosei has superb coastal walks to hidden coves. In the southeast, picturesque bays, lagoons and long stretches of sandy beaches and dunes alternate with craggy promontories and cliffs plunging into the sea. And in the southwest, it is a delight to walk along the coastline punctuated with watchtowers.

ALGHERO TO BOSA

This gloriously undulating 42km stretch of coastal road skirts little coves and swathes of golden-white sands. It's also a popular cycling route, best done over a couple of days giving plenty of time to cool off in the sparkling seas. You may even be lucky enough to spot the endangered griffon vulture – Italy's largest colony of these enormous birds is here.

CYCLING

You can hire bicycles in several of the bigger towns and coastal resorts and, for seriously challenging terrain, in the mountainous areas of the Gennargentu. Inland from Ólbia, the extraordinary moonscape of the Valle della Luna is superb cycling territory. Generally, there are fantastic opportunities for on- and off-road cycling throughout the island. Inclines can be severe and often very demanding, but the scenery is breathtaking – literally – and worth the effort. Online, visit www.sardiniabybike.cjb.net for some suggested itineraries.

Exploring the Sínis Peninsula by bicycle

WILDLIFE

Everywhere you go in the interior you'll hear the sound of sheep and goats' bells. Small and hardy, they are the island's most prolific residents. But, as a remote island, there are many rare species too, such as the mouflon – the long-horned wild sheep that is on the brink of extinction on mainland Italy. Not far from Su Nuraxi, Giara di Gesturi is home to *cavallini* – miniature wild horses. The island of Asinara is famous for its unique little albino donkeys. And, if you're very lucky, you might spot a *cervo sardo* (Sardinian deer) roaming in the Gennargentu mountains.

Known sometimes as the Island of Winds (l'Ísola del Vento), the offshore breezes carry cargoes of visiting birds. Sardinia is home to 200 different species – a third of the entire number found in Europe – many of which come for the rich pickings of succulent shrimps in the lagoons. And many like it so much that they have changed their migratory habits, such as the colonies of pink flamingoes that are now nesting and breeding in the lagoons.

Endemic to Sardinia are rare birds such as the golden eagle, peregrine falcon and Eleonora's falcon. The sea teems with marine flora and fauna and rich, red coral around the coast of Alghero. Dolphins are often sighted around the Maddalena islands, and the Golfo di Orosei is reputed to be the last home of the monk seal (*bue marino*), although these endangered creatures are very elusive nowadays.

Bright Sardinian flora: thistles (below) and mesembryanthemums (bottom)

FLORA

Throughout the year, but especially in spring and autumn, the island is ablaze with flowers. Roses and thick carpets of vivid magenta daisy-like mesembryanthemums open their petals to greet the sun; the latter are nicknamed '*buon giorno*' flowers. And all are intertwined with exotic orchids, hibiscus, oleander and swathes of bougainvillaea. A thick mantle of *macchia mediterranea* (Mediterranean maquis) covers most of the land. This tangled profusion of lavender, rosemary, wild fennel, herbs, and plants such as juniper, myrtle and strawberry tree is richly colourful and highly fragrant.

21

What's On

FEBRUARY/MARCH

Carnevale: Carnival is celebrated throughout the island but Sa Sartiglia in Oristano is an extraordinary medieval joust of horsemen in glorious traditional costume. In Mamoiada, the *mamuthones* process in sinister wooden masks and heavy sheepskin cloaks.

APRIL

28 Apr: Sa Die de Sa Sardigna, Sardinia Day, commemorates the Vesper Insurrection (Vespri Sardi) of 1794, which eventually led to the expulsion of the Piedmontese from Sardinia. There's a re-enactment in San Remy of the arrest of the revolt leaders, and musical shows continue late into the night.

MAY

1–4 May: One of Sardinia's most colourful festivals takes place in Cágliari to honour Sant'Efisio, the island's patron saint.
Cavalcata Sarda: On the penultimate Sunday in May, Sássari stages a costumed pageant celebrating a victory over the Saracens in AD1000, followed by a spirited horseback gallop through the streets.

JULY

6–8 Jul: S'Ardia takes place in Sedilo – a spectacular but dangerous horse race between Oristano and Núoro, accompanied by gunshots and thousands of spectators.

AUGUST

14 Aug: Sássari celebrates I Candelieri, when giant timber candles are paraded through the streets in the city's biggest feast.
29 Aug: Monte Ortobene celebrates Sagra del Redentore, marked by a torch-lit procession and fabulous traditional costumes.

SEPTEMBER

Festa di San Salvatore: On the first Sunday of the month there's an 8km barefoot race to San Salvatore from Cábras, and back again the next day.

OCTOBER

Sagra delle Castagne: Chestnut fair held on the last Sunday at Aritzo in the Barbágia.

DECEMBER

Christmas: Christmas Day is a feast day in Sardinia, but not the major commercial event it is in many Western countries.

SARDINIA'S
top 25 sights

The sights are shown on the maps on the inside front cover and inside back cover, numbered **1**–**25** alphabetically

Alghero

INFORMATION

🚦 B1

✉ 11km southeast from
Alghero-Fertília airport

🍴 Numerous cafés/
restaurants (€–€€€)

🚌 Regular FdS buses from
airport to Piazza della
Mercede

♿ Good

🔄 Grotta di Nettuno
(➤ 31), Sássari (➤ 42)

*Display of coral jewellery
in a shop window,
Alghero*

**Bathed in a warm coral glow, Alghero
sits on a peninsula surrounded by
towers and fortifications, and is the
heart of the Coral Riviera.**

The town has a distinct Catalan character as a
result of Catalan colonisation in the 14th century.
Elegant Spanish-style arches bridge the streets,
festooned with laundry. The shops, too, are
festooned with coral jewellery and carvings, for
which the town is famous.

The busiest lane in the tangle of lanes in the
medieval Old Town is the Via Carlo Alberto,
studded with shops and bars. But for less
sybaritic interest there are the two churches –
San Michele and San Francesco. The former
dominates the skyline with its glistening
ceramic dome and is perhaps the most opulent
of the Jesuits' baroque churches on the island.

San Francesco, halfway along, is
also one of Alghero's landmarks. It
is a blend of Gothic, Romanesque
and Renaissance with parts of the
cloisters dating to the 13th century.
On summer evenings concerts are
staged in the magical setting.

Alghero's other famous
ecclesiastical landmark is the
Cattedrale. Dating from the 16th
century, the interior is a mixture of
architectural styles, but there are
some magnificent examples of
marble, as well as the impressive
dome, added in the 18th century.
It's also possible to take tours of
the campanile in the summer.

The waterfront is girded by the
bastoni (walls) and a walk along
here towards the port is the perfect
spot for an evening stroll, or
passeggiata.

Arcipélago de La Maddalena

A cluster of dreamy islands with Caribbean-blue seas make up the archipelago off the northeast coast, near the Costa Smeralda.

The only inhabited island is La Maddalena itself, from where there is a causeway to Garibaldi's island, Caprera (► 32). But the other five main islands (► 50–51) can be seen on boat trips, including Budelli with its glorious pale pink beach, Spiaggia Rosa.

Rocks hewn over thousands of years characterise the landscape of the Gallura region, and on La Maddalena there are about 150 of them whose shape has earned them nicknames from the locals – such as Rabbit Rock, Eagle's Beak, De Gaulle, Dinosaur, and even '*Il Mostro di Lochness*' (Loch Ness monster).

La Maddalena town is a bustling place with cobbled streets and piazzas, and a decorous *passeggiata* along the Via Garibaldi, the main street that connects Piazza Umberto I to Piazza Garibaldi. There are some good restaurants around the squares and pleasant bars in which to people watch. The Museo Diocesano in the heart of town has some fascinating exhibits, including two silver candlesticks and a crucifix gifted by Lord Horatio Nelson.

On the road to Cala Spalmatore (about 1km out of town) is the Museo Archeológico Navale on the Via Panoramica. The main exhibits are of a Roman cargo ship that was wrecked in the waters of the archipelago around 120BC, showing a reconstructed cross-section of the hull, and amphorae, most of which contained wine.

The archipelago was declared a national park in 1996. Controversially, the US Navy established a nuclear submarine base on Ísola Santo Stefano in 1973, during the Cold War. At President Renato Soru's behest, the base was closed in 2008.

INFORMATION

- A3
- Off the northeast coast
- Bars and restaurants (€–€€)
- Limited
- Regular ferries depart from Palau to La Maddalena, or from Cannigione and Santa Teresa in the summer
- Arzachena (► 26), Costa Smeralda (► 29), Santa Teresa di Gallura (► 41, 53)

Beautifully maintained house façade in La Maddalena

Arzachena Prehistoric Sites

INFORMATION

➕ A3

✉ 26km from Ólbia

🕐 Jul–Sep daily 9–8;
Easter–Jun, Oct daily 9–1,
3–7

🏛 Moderate

🚌 Regular buses from Ólbia
take 45 minutes; limited
service from Santa Teresa
di Gallura

♿ None

🔁 Arcipélago de La
Maddalena (➤ 25, 50),
Costa Smeralda (➤ 29),
Porto Cervo (➤ 53),
Ólbia (➤ 39), Santa
Teresa di Gallura
(➤ 41, 53)

Away from the coast, discover giants' tombs and megalithic stone circles in the prehistoric remains dotted in the woods and fields around Arzachena.

Among olive groves, myrtle and prickly pear, the Nuraghe Albucciu, 2km southeast of Arzachena, is one of Gallura's best-preserved *nuraghi*. It has an unusual granite roof that is flat rather than conical. About 4km south of Arzachena is Coddu Vecchiu (also known as Coddhu' Ecchju) – one of the island's most complete 'giants' tombs'. The original corridor tomb is estimated to date to the 18th–16th centuries BC, and it was extended in Nuraghic times by adding a forecourt edged by stone, used for various rites – probably including sacrifices.

Nearby are the Tomba dei Giganti di Li Lolghi and Necropoli di Li Muri. Regarded as Gallura's finest example, Tomba dei Giganti di Li Lolghi rises on a hillock and, although similar to Coddu Vecchiu, is nearly twice as long in the inner chamber.

The Necropolis of Li Muri is reached by returning on the rough track to the left fork going west off the track from the road signposted Luogosanto. This burial site is estimated to date back to 3500BC and consists of several rectangular tombs of stone slabs

The distinctive mushroom-shaped rock of Arzachena

encircled by smaller slabs. There are five central circles that contained bodies buried in a crouching position. Beside each tomb there are standing stones (menhirs) – some of which have fallen over – and small stone boxes for sacrifices.

Although a useful base, the town of Arzachena itself doesn't merit a long visit, but the natural rock sculpture Roccia Il Fungo (Mushroom Rock) is worth a look at the end of Via Limbara.

Cágliari

Sardinia's capital Cágliari is a proud, salty port – the island's largest city by far – and a tantalising pot-pourri of ancient and modern.

INFORMATION

➕ D2

✉ On south coast

🚌 Bus from airport to Piazza Matteotti (10 minutes)

♿ Castello has steep access but there are lifts

❓ Parking can be a problem. Car parks by the waterfront are the best option

🔄 Nora (➤ 36), Poetto (➤ 52)

Known as Casteddu ('the castle') in the Sardinian language, Cágliari perches on top of a hill overlooking its beautiful gulf – the Bay of Angels. Most of the white limestone city walls are intact and the impressive effect of the warm Mediterranean sunlight reflecting on the dazzling city moved D. H. Lawrence to compare the city to a 'white Jerusalem' in his book *Sea and Sardinia*. The Castello quarter is the old town and houses the most important artistic treasures of the city in the Citadella dei Musei – the highlight of which is the Museo Archeológico Nazionale. This is the island's most important collection of artefacts from prehistoric to Nuraghic, Phoenician, Carthaginian and Roman times (➤ 58).

The Castello district overlooks the Largo Carlo Felice, Cágliari's most important street, where the fragrant jacaranda trees put on a breathtaking floral display. At the southern end of this wide boulevard is the Via Roma, lined with cafés, bars and elegant shops and the place to watch the evening *passeggiata*. Behind it is the characterful Marina district, bursting with speciality shops and excellent restaurants. This is the perfect place for strolling and dining in the maze of little streets behind the Via Roma.

Shuttered windows, ornate balconies and peeling paintwork are typical of Cágliari houses

The city outskirts may be sprawling and industrial but even there flamingos preen and birdlife flocks in to the lagoons, not so far from the airport itself.

Castelsardo

INFORMATION

➕ A2

✉ 32km northeast of Sássari

🚌 Frequent buses from Sássari (1 hour)

♿ Poor; no wheelchair access to castle

🔄 Sássari (► 42)

Castello and Museo dell'Intreccio Mediterraneo

🕐 Jul–Aug daily 9am–midnight; Sep 9–1, 3–9; reduced hours at other times

💷 Inexpensive

Looking up at Castelsardo's imposing ramparts

Originally Genoese, this picturesque and popular town stands sentinel over the northwestern coast on its rocky outcrop.

Northeast of Sássari, the imposing medieval citadel of Castelsardo perches high on its cliff with a jumble of houses at its feet. The view from the coastal road SS200 is spectacular. Originally known as Castelgenovese in the 12th century, then Castelaragonese by the mid-15th century, the castle has made this coastal town very popular even though its strategic importance has long since disappeared. The town is famous for its handicrafts and the castle has an excellent museum (Museo dell'Intreccio Mediterraneo) devoted to *l'intreccio* (straw-weaving), used not only for baskets but also ropes, huts and boats. The shops are full of *intreccio* items made from straw, reeds, raffia, wicker, asphodel leaves and the authentic dwarf-palm leaves, locally picked around Castelsardo.

Other handicrafts worth seeking out are ceramic and cork and the scary Sard wooden masks. The main sights are in the Old Town up the steep steps and streets where, as well as the castle, the Cattedrale di Sant'Antonio Abate is worth a look. From the top of the castle there are splendid views – you can see right across to Corsica on a clear day. The old fishing port is still active and there is a small town beach lined with shops, bars and restaurants. Castelsardo is also famous for its seafood – especially lobster and mussels.

Costa Smeralda

The waters of the Emerald Coast sparkle like a jewel, reflected in the diamonds and platinum of those who flock to this 'millionaires' playground'.

In the 1950s the Aga Khan discovered this 10km coastal strip of unadulterated nature, fell in love with the sandy beaches and idyllic coves and made it an exclusive resort. But the charms of this coastline are not just confined to the 'Smeralda', there are gorgeous beaches and bays all around where you don't have to worry about seriously denting your credit card.

The Costa Smeralda extends just 10km between the Golfo di Cugnana and Golfo di Arzachena, but has an extraordinarily beautiful 56km coastline. The Aga Khan's former consortium was sold to American property group Colony Capital in 2003, although the Starwood hotel group still manages the major hotels. The area has stuck firmly by the guiding principle that all development should blend into the superb scenery without disfiguring it in any way. Consequently there are no high-rise buildings, telephone wires and electrical cables have to be hidden underground, and the buildings are a curious mix of troglodyte-Moroccan styles.

Porto Cervo is the only real town and 'capital' of the area. Disguised as a Mediterranean fishing village, it's a pleasant place to stroll, to see and be seen – and to window shop. Beware, the designer shops in the Piazzetta don't make a habit of displaying their prices. It all tends to be very quiet in the day as everyone is on their yacht, relaxing in their villa or on the beach. The best time to visit is at sunset and later.

The Porto Cervo marina is one of the world's best and home to the Mediterranean's most beautiful and biggest boats. There are many regattas and races staged here, including the Settimana delle Bocche at the end of August.

INFORMATION

- ⊞ A3
- ✉ 12km north of Ólbia
- ♨ Many cafés and restaurants, especially on the Piazzetta (€€€)
- 🚌 Regular buses from Ólbia and Porto Cervo
- ❓ Numerous beaches and coves accessed by rough tracks
- ↔ Aquadream Water Park (➤ 57), Arcipélago de La Maddalena (➤ 25), Arzachena (➤ 26), Golfo Aranci (➤ 52), Ólbia (➤ 39), Porto Cervo beaches (➤ 53)

Idyllic whitewashed villas are dotted about the Costa Smeralda

Golfo di Orosei

- B3
- 40km east of Núoro
- Restaurants and bars (€–€€€), even on remote beaches in high summer
- Shuttle buses from Dorgali (20 minutes)
- Cala Gonone (➤ 51), Dorgali (➤ 54, 59), Monte Ortobene (➤ 19), Núoro (➤ 55), Tiscali (➤ 46)

Grotta del Bue Marino

- ☎ 078 496243
- Aug visits at 9, 10, 11, 12, 3, 4, 5; Jul 9, 10, 11, 12, 3; Easter–Jun, Sep–Oct 11, 3
- Boat trips from Cala Gonone include the Grotta and other beaches,
- Poor

Limestone cliffs and rock formations along the Gulf's coast are punctuated by beautiful coves, secluded grottos and fabulous hidden beaches.

The Gulf of Orosei is a symmetrical arch extending 40km from Capo Nero in the north to Capo Monte Santo in the south. It is the seafront of the Supramonte – a wild and steep coast where holm oak forests, centuries-old juniper trees and *macchia* extend down to the sea. The royal eagle, Eleonora's falcon and griffon vulture are regular residents and these birds of prey can often be seen peeping out from their eyries on the clifftops. And further inland, herds of mouflon are often encountered.

South of Orosei town, Cala Gonone has a gorgeous setting around a harbour framed by soaring mountains. Once a little fishing village populated by Neapolitan fisherfolk who had come over from the island of Ponza, it started to develop as a tourist resort when the famous Grotta del Bue Marino opened in the 1950s. This is one of Sardinia's most spectacular caves – the largest and most dramatically beautiful of the many grottos on this coast.

The *bue marino* (sea-ox) is the local name for the monk seal, common a century ago on many Mediterranean islands, but now one of the world's most endangered mammals. This cave was one of their last hiding places in Sardinia, although the last sightings were back in 1992.

Cala Gonone itself has good beaches, all within walking distance from the harbour. Other beaches such as Cala Fuili, Cala Cartoe and Cala Luna, considered to be some of the most beautiful in world, are all within a few kilometres of the harbour. Accessible by boat, the coves are surrounded by crystal clear waters, offering wonderful swimming and snorkelling opportunities.

The spectacular setting of Cala Gonone

Grotta di Nettuno

Neptune's Grotto extends 2.5km into the limestone promontory of Capo Cáccia, which has been sculpted by waves and the wind for millennia.

Around the headland is the spectacular, giddying Escala del Cabirol (meaning 'goat's steps' in Catalan). This 654-step descent leads to the famous Grotta di Nettuno.

The stunning deep cavern with a lake is known as Neptune's Grotto, the mythical abode of nymphs. It is filled with stalactites and stalagmites, twisted into fantastical shapes – a subterranean fairyland that appears to be populated by human figures, statues, trees and animals. All is bathed in colour ranging from greenish-blue to white, yellow and orange crystals reflected by the shimmering phosphorescence of the rock.

A tour of the Grotto takes you 200m around the shores of a saltwater lake, Lamarmora, facing the Acquasantiera – or holy water font – a huge 2m-high stalagmite. As the natural light ends and the darkness begins, shapes such as the Great Organ eerily seem to come to life. Guides fondly remember when visitors could row across the lake, lit by thousands of small candles on small plates floated on the water, creating an otherworldly glow of enchantment in the grand chamber. Let your imagination run free with the enchanting spectacle of those tiny, quivering flames throwing shadows on the wall and the reflections in the still waters of the lake.

INFORMATION

- 🚩 B1
- ✉ Capo Cáccia, 24km west of Alghero
- ☎ 079 946540
- ◉ Guided tours every hour: Apr–Sep daily 9–7; Oct 9–5; Jan–Mar, Nov–Dec 9–4 (weather permitting)
- 🍴 Bar at the top of the steps (€€)
- 🚌 Jun–Sep bus from Alghero at 9.15, 3, 10, 5.10 and from Capo Cáccia at noon, 4.05, 6.05; Oct–May from Alghero 9.15 and from Capo Cáccia at noon
- 🚢 From Alghero hourly in summer, mornings only in winter
- ♿ No wheelchair access
- 💷 Expensive
- 🔄 Alghero (➤ 24)

Vertiginous descent to the Grotta di Nettuno

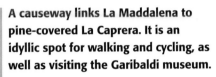

Ísola Caprera

INFORMATION

🔲 A3
✉ Off northeast coast
🚢 Regular ferries to
   La Maddalena from Palau
♿ Limited
❓ Car park next to the
   museum
🔄 Arcipélago de La
   Maddalena (▶ 25, 50)

Museo Garibaldino
🕐 Jun–Sep Tue–Sun 9–1.30,
   4–6.30; Oct–May 9–1.30
🍴 Shop sells cold drinks
🎫 Moderate

*The cool white buildings
of the Museo Garibaldino*

A causeway links La Maddalena to pine-covered La Caprera. It is an idyllic spot for walking and cycling, as well as visiting the Garibaldi museum.

This woody, undeveloped island is a wildlife sanctuary protected by stringent building restrictions. Revolutionary Giuseppe Garibaldi (1807–82) (▶ 34) chose it as his home for the last third of his life – perhaps in the belief that paradise was not so different from this.

In the courtyard of his house stands a majestic pine planted by Garibaldi on the day his daughter Celia was born (he had seven children by three wives and one by a governess). He was an agronomist, and set up a farm with vegetable gardens and an olive mill.

The house, Casa Bianca, has changed little since his death. His personal effects include his red shirt (*camicia rossa*) – famous as his troops were known as the Red Shirts – and two embroidered fez hats, another trademark. The rooms are small and simple, with the exception of his more spacious death chamber. Built at the request of his wife, Francesca, it looks out to the Straits of Bonifacio and Corsica and towards Nice, the city of his birth. In this room the calendar shows the date of his death, Friday, 2 June 1882.

His tomb in the garden is made of rough granite, in total contrast with the grandiose marble tombs of five of his children and his last wife.

Ísola di San Pietro

This island off the southwest coast was named after St. Peter, who was marooned here during a storm. Today it is a little piece of paradise.

As the first sight of Carloforte, the island's only town, comes into view, you could easily imagine yourself to be on the Italian Riviera in mainland Liguria. Pastel-coloured houses cluster around the harbour and little alleys and the main street bears the name Via Genova. None of this is surprising when you discover that a colony of Genoese coral fishermen came here to settle in 1738 and a version of the old Genoese language is still spoken today.

Fishing boats bob in the harbour and the little houses are surrounded by pine forest, vineyards and a profusion of flowers. San Pietro is the perfect place for strolling, relaxing, taking a boat trip around the dramatic coastline and Punta delle Colonne rock formations that stand like sentinels guarding this beautiful island. It's perfect, too, for dining in one of the very good restaurants where seafood and fish are the stars. Try the locally caught *tonno* (tuna) or *pesce spada* (swordfish). Other famous Ligurian-Sardinian specialities include *pesto carlofortino*, made with basil, pine nuts, parmesan, garlic, olive oil and tomatoes.

INFORMATION

➕ D1
✉ Off southwest coast
🍴 Many restaurants
    (€€–€€€)
🚢 Regular ferries from
    Calasetta on Sant'Antioco
    (30 minutes)

Rock stack at Punta delle Colonne off the south coast of San Pietro

Ísola Tavolara

Rising like a knife-edge above the sea, this limestone mountain is home to rare birds, including peregrine falcons, and, surprisingly, to royalty.

Measuring 4km long by 1km wide, this island – part of a protected Marine Park – lies just to the south of Ólbia and is dominated by its imposing rock towering 564m above the Tyrrhenian Sea. The eastern side of Tavolara is a military zone, but there's free access to the inhabited western side, which even has a cemetery. In here are the tombs of Tavolara's 'kings', as Tavolara was once one of the smallest kingdoms on the planet.

After King Carlo Alberto of Sardinia visited the island in 1833 for a spot of goat hunting and feasting, he gratefully 'crowned' his host, Giuseppe Bertoleoni, as an independent sovereign monarch. On Giuseppe's death, his eldest son became King Paolo and since that time the island's kings have all descended from the Bertoleoni family, recognized as the rulers of Tavolara by the kings of Sardinia. The present sovereign, Carlo II of Tavolara, is an Italian citizen named Tonino Bertoleoni, who runs the Da Tonino restaurant on the island.

The arms of the kingdom and island display a walrus sitting on a rock. While you won't see any of these creatures, wild goats still roam and it is a paradise for birds, including eagles and peregrine falcons. On the southern tip there's a good beach at Spalmatore di Terra, where there are some eateries and bars (open in summer). Tavolara is the unlikely setting for an annual film festival in mid-July, when non-mainsream Italian films are screened on the beach (visit www.cinematavolara.it).

On the Sardinian mainland, the small fishing village of Porto San Paolo is directly across a small strait from Ísola Tavolara, and from here there are regular sailings to the island.

Monti del Gennargentu

Meaning 'silver gate', the Gennargentu is the highest mountain range in Sardinia and is covered with silver – in the form of snow – in winter.

This is the heart of Sardinia, also known as Barbágia; it was originally dubbed 'Barbaria' by the Romans, as Emperor Tiberius sent in troops of hardened criminals and political prisoners to combat the assaults of bandits and herdsmen from the Gennargentu, but to no avail. This area remains unconquered.

Today the image of mountain bandits is still bolstered by some fanciful tourist literature, but in reality, new roads and communications have tamed those antisocial scenarios, although sheep rustling continues and, doubtless, vendettas are still waged, but quietly.

There are many villages dotted around that were originally home to shepherds and their flocks. Sardinia's highest village is Fonni, lying at 1,000m above sea level and popular with both walkers and skiers – mostly the cross-country variety but with a little modest downhill skiing, too. The highest peaks are all accessible from here: Bruncu Spina at 1,829m and Punta La Mármora at 1,834m. From the top of Punta La Mármora, there are fabulous views over the entire island to reward you for the strenuous climb. For a less energetic foray, it is possible to drive most of the way up to Bruncu Spina to the S'Arena *rifugio* (mountain refuge) at 1,500m, from where it's a relatively easy hike to the top.

The area is still thickly vegetated with holm oak woods surrounded by *macchia*. The lower flanks of the Gennargentu are cloaked in vineyards that produce the famous red wine made from the Cannonau grape, and this area is also especially noted for pecorino cheese. Along the coastal cliffs, olive trees, carob trees and juniper thrive in the warm climate.

INFORMATION

- ➕ C2
- ✉ Núoro province
- 🚌 Limited bus service from Núoro to mountain villages
- ❓ Walking in the Gennargentu you will come across many *pinnette* (huts with thatched roofs) still used by shepherds for shelter

Rugged-looking cows roam the mountain meadows

Nora

INFORMATION

✚ D2
✉ 30km southwest of Cágliari
🚌 Regular shuttle buses from Pula to Nora
↔ Cágliari (► 27, 58)

Zona Archeológica
🕐 Daily 9–7.30
♿ Moderate (ticket also gives admission to Museo Archeológico in Pula)

Black, white and tan mosaic in the remains of a patrician villa

The coastal city of Nora was the first on the island to be founded by the Phoenicians in the 8th century BC.

Strategically positioned on the Capo di Pula promontory, it had three harbours, so ensuring that at least one of them would be sheltered from the winds. The Carthaginians arrived in the 6th century BC, followed by the Romans, who expanded it to become the most important city in Sardinia. But its demise began in the 5th century AD with attacks by pirates and Vandals, while rising seas led to the submergence of a third of the site.

Nowadays it is an evocative place, encircled by fragrant umbrella pines and overlooking a pretty beach. After entering the archaeological zone you come to a single column from the Temple of Tanit – the Carthaginian goddess of fertility. Most of the remains date to the Roman period, including the theatre facing the sea, which was the only one that staged plays rather than entertainment of the gladiatorial variety in Roman times (it is still used for open-air concerts in summer).

Other highlights are the Thermae – baths – of which there are the remains of four of different sizes, used for people of different social classes. There are also some fine mosaic floors, especially in the remains of a patrician villa and the Forum.

En route to Nora you pass through the busy town of Pula, which is full of shops, bars and eateries, and an archaeological museum with finds from Nora's excavations.

Nuraghe Losa

Inland there are many traces of the Nuraghic culture, and one of the most impressive examples is Nuraghe Losa.

Just a few kilometres west of the Carlo Felice highway (SS131), this huge megalithic monument looms into view. It is one of Sardinia's most important and best-preserved Nuraghic monuments. Encircled by two large walls – the inner one with small towers – it is built of great basalt blocks and is estimated to be more than 3,500 years old.

The *nuraghe* has a truncated cone or beehive shape, built in the distinctive Cyclopean style, which used no mortar – nor any other binding material – but was erected entirely by piling up huge blocks. The central tower, 13m high and 12.5m wide, originally had three floors and almost certainly a crenellated top, long gone.

A narrow stone corridor gives access to two of the original three storeys of the topless central tower and several ancillary buildings dotted around the site. The interior is illuminated by sunken lighting and the walls are peppered with niches and alcoves. Around it are later towers, enclosed in an imposing triangular curtain and surrounded and fortified by defensive walls estimated to date to around the 7th century BC. Winding stone steps lead up to a terrace from where there are splendid views over the high plain and as far as Gennargentu on a clear day.

The exact origins and functions of these monuments are unclear. However, as *losa* means 'tomb' in Sardinian dialect, it may have been a mausoleum. There is evidence of a prehistoric village around the perimeter wall and, inside the main entrance, cinerary urns from the first to 2nd century AD. The village was continuously occupied from the middle Bronze Age to the 7th century AD. This peaceful yet eerie site is the perfect place to let your imagination roam.

INFORMATION

- B2
- 30km northeast of Oristano
- 0785 53402
- Summer 9–5
- Abbasanta, followed by 3km walk
- Not suitable
- Moderate
- Fordongiánus (➤ 55), Oristano (➤ 40)
- There is a small museum here with a few artefacts, but the major finds are in Cágliari's archaeological museum (➤ 58)

Looking up inside the central tower

Nuraghe Su Nuraxi

INFORMATION

➕ C2

✉ Su Nuraxi, Barúmini

☎ 070 936 8128

🕐 Daily 9–dusk. Entry by guided tour only (usually multilingual), running on the half-hour

🍴 Snack bar opposite entrance (€)

🚌 Infrequent bus from Cágliari

♿ Not suitable for wheelchair users. The terrain is very uneven

💰 Expensive

🔁 Parco Sardegna in Miniatura (➤ 57)

In Sardinian dialect, 'su nuraxi' means simply 'the nuraghi' and this Unesco World Heritage Site is the largest Nuraghic complex on the island.

The complex at Barúmini, which was extended and reinforced by the Carthaginians, is the finest and most complete example of this remarkable form of prehistoric architecture. Visible for miles around, the main central tower of Su Nuraxi towers over a small plain, surrounded by other *nuraghi* in a star-shaped pattern. Yet for centuries it was buried among the hills of the Marmilla area. Excavation only began in 1949 and still continues today.

The oldest section is the huge three-storey central tower that was originally 18m high and is now 13.7m. It is estimated to date back to 1500BC and is thought to have been buried by the Sards and Carthaginians during the time of the Roman conquest. What remains today is remarkably well preserved.

Built of dark basalt blocks, the central tower is believed to have been constructed from volcanic stone transported from 10km away. The complexity of Nuraghic constructions varied greatly, depending on the function and importance of the buildings. Here, the fortress had a bastion with four towers at the corners. These led to the courtyard through long corridors. The lower chamber at the end of a corridor is of the *tholos* type – where a 'false cupola' is built by laying successive stones so that each course overhangs the previous one. To get here you have to negotiate narrow, dim passageways and steps hewn from the rock. From the top there are superb views of the whole site and of the 200-plus horse-shoe-shaped roofless buildings of the surrounding Nuraghic village, some of which have now been reconstructed.

The central tower at Su Nuraxi

Ólbia

The capital of Gallura, Ólbia is the gateway to the beautiful beaches of the northeast coast and the glittering Costa Smeralda.

Despite its Greek name, meaning 'happy', Ólbia's origins were Phoenician before the town became a Roman trading post. Today it is Sardinia's busiest passenger port and has an international airport. Although there are few vestiges of its former glory as one of Sardinia's oldest cities, the Basilica di San Simplicio is Gallura's most important medieval church. The giant Tavolara limestone rock towers over the bay – a favourite with peregrine falcons and a place of 'kings' (► 34).

On arrival at Ólbia you could be forgiven for being happy to get out of it as quickly as possible – it is busy, traffic-choked and full of roadworks and diversions. However, the cobbled lanes in the old part of town around the Corso Umberto are full of good restaurants and some pretty piazzas to linger in over a drink. From here, past the level crossing and the railway station, you come to the town's top tourist sight, the Basilica di San Simplicio.

This 11th- to 12th-century Pisan Romanesque church is hewn out of Galluran granite and its façade, although austere, is very handsome. Inside there are columns and other pieces of masonry such as funerary urns that were salvaged from pagan Phoenician and Roman temples. In the apse there are two 13th-century frescoes, the left-hand one of which depicts San Simplicio, the patron saint of Ólbia. The Festa di San Simplicio, Ólbia's biggest festival, is celebrated for three days in mid-May every year with processions, dancing, poetry recitals, fireworks and feasting.

INFORMATION

- ✚ A3
- ✉ Northeast Sardinia
- 🍴 Many bars and restaurants around Corso Umberto (€€)
- 🚌 2, 10 from airport to Piazza Regina Margherita
- 🚊 Regular trains from Sássari and Cágliari
- ↔ Arzachena (► 26), Costa Smeralda (► 29, 53), Golfo Aranci (► 52), Ísola Tavolara (► 34)

Basilica di San Simplicio
- ✉ Via Simplicio
- 🕐 Daily 9–12.30, 4–7 (times can be variable)

Fishing boats moored in Ólbia's harbour

Oristano

INFORMATION

✛ C1
✉ 95km northwest of
Cágliari
🍴 Numerous bars and
restaurants (€–€€)
🚌 Regular buses from
Cágliari and Sássari
↔ Monte Ferru (➤ 61),
Nuraghe Losa (➤ 37),
Sínis Peninsula (➤ 43),
Thárros (➤ 45)

Antiquarium Arborense
✉ Piazzetta Corrias
☎ 0783 791262
🕐 Daily 9–2, 3–8
💶 Moderate

Duomo
✉ Piazza Duomo
🕐 Apr–Oct daily 8–1, 4–7;
Nov–Mar 7–1, 3–6.30
💶 Moderate

The Duomo's campanile

Sardinia's fourth provincial capital may be one of the lesser-known towns on the island but is very rewarding, with a particulary good archaeology museum.

The city enjoys a striking location, lying at the northern end of the fertile Campidano plain, surrounded by lagoons and only 5km from the sea. Nearby the ancient Phoenician-Roman site of Thárros (➤ 45) is spectacularly set at the tip of the Sínis Peninsula (➤ 43), which is perfect not only for its historical sites but also for its good beaches and wealth of birdlife.

'Città della ceramica' is the sign that welcomes you to Oristano, as the town is famous for its ceramics. It is also the site of the colourful Sa Sartiglia festival, held during Carnival on Sunday and *martedí grasso* (mardi gras) in Piazza Eleonora d'Arborea.

The Piazza Roma is at the heart of town with its medieval tower, Torre di Mariano II, also known as San Cristoforo. The tower is a unique remnant of the city walls to which it was joined and which were destroyed at the end of the 19th century.

The best sight is the town's Antiquarium Arborense, just southeast of Piazza Roma. This is home to one of the island's top archaeological collections with displays spanning prehistoric, Nuraghic, Phoenician and Roman treasures. On the ground floor a 4th-century BC lion from Thárros greets you.

The Duomo (cathedral) is the largest in Sardinia and is devoted to Santa Maria Assunta. Although founded in the 12th century, its current baroque style is the result of its 18th-century reconstruction. The onion-domed campanile is a symbol of the Oristano skyline.

Santa Teresa di Gallura

Lying right on the northernmost tip of the island, this is a very popular summer resort with glorious views over the Straits of Bonifacio to the island of Corsica.

The town is arranged on a grid system and at its heart is the Piazza Vittorio Emanuele, which is full of pastel-coloured houses, bars and cafés. From here the Via del Mare leads to the 16th-century Torre di Langosardo Spanish watch-tower, where you can drink in the glorious views towards the cliffs of Corsica. A path leads west of the tower to the main beach, Spiaggia Rena Bianca. This is the town beach, just a stone's throw from the centre, with turquoise sea and flour-fine sand. It is also extremely popular in high season.

Some 4km to the west, the granite headland Capo Testa has two beaches: the one on the left-hand side has crystalline waters and soft sand that shelves gently, making it ideal for children, while the beach on the right has amazing rock formations.

Santa Teresa has a vibrant nightlife and has established itself as one of the region's top buzzing bar scenes. The waters and lovely beaches around here (➤ 53) also attract many wind- and kite-surfers, and the annual Kitesurfing World Cup is held here at the end of September.

INFORMATION

- ➕ A2
- ✉ 61km northwest of Ólbia
- 🍴 Numerous bars and restaurants (€–€€)
- 🚌 Regular buses from Ólbia
- 🚢 Saremar and Mobyline run regular services to Bonifacio; excursions also to La Maddalena and Costa Smeralda
- 🔄 Arcipélago de La Maddalena (➤ 25, 50)

Windsurfer off Capo Testa

41

Sássari

INFORMATION

✚ B1

✉ 30km northeast of Alghero-Fertilia airport

🍴 Numerous bars and restaurants (€–€€€)

🚌 Many buses from Alghero and Oristano

🚆 Direct trains from Cágliari (4.25 hours)

🔗 Alghero (➤ 24), Castelsardo (➤ 28), Museo Nazionale Sanna (➤ 58), Valle dei Nuraghi (➤ 47)

Chiesa di Santa Maria di Betlem

✉ Piazza di Santa Maria

🕐 Daily 7.15–12, 5–8

The ornate façade of the Duomo di San Nicola

After Cágliari, this sophisticated university town is Sardinia's second city – although the Sassarese will tell you it's the first.

At the core of the historic centre, the Duomo di San Nicola stands on a site where archaeological research has revealed traces of a pre-existing building from Roman times. What you see today is a baroque fantasy façade, added in the 18th century, very reminiscent of Lecce baroque from Puglia in the south of Italy. Around here, the lively narrow streets of the medieval town are perfect for a stroll. Inevitably, you end up at the Corso Vittorio Emanuele II. This street is full of gorgeous *palazzi* – some crumbling, others restored. Along here, the lovely Liberty-style Teatro Cívico has been beautifully restored and the jewel-box interior is like a miniature version of Milan's La Scala opera house. This is where the local dignitaries meet before the Candelieri procession on 14 August (➤ 22).

Along Corso Trinità are remnants of the city's medieval walls and the Fontana di Rosello – a splendid Renaissance fountain in marble and dark stone. At Piazza di Santa Maria, close to the site of the orginal city walls, is the Chiesa di Santa Maria di Betlem. Founded in 1106, it has a lovely Romanesque façade, while the inside is more overblown baroque. The lateral chapels display the *candelieri* (giant wooden candles) that represent the town's medieval craft guilds and are paraded for the Candelieri festival. Made from wood and polychrome, they are about 420cm tall and weigh about 310kg.

All roads lead to the heart of town on the Piazza Italia – a building site at the time of writing, due to reopen in 2009. Still, a stroll along the Via Roma just off the Piazza is always a delight, and this is the centre of Sássari's thriving café society.

Sínis Peninsula

This low-lying peninsula west of Oristano is a watery wonderland full of the island's largest lagoons and regularly visited by migrating birds.

It is famous, too, for the coracle-style *fassoni* boats made of rushes and used by the local fishermen to catch the bounty of these waters. While they silently net the mullet and eel, the peace is broken only by the honking of the ruddy shelduck, indigenous to this lagoon, but already extinct in mainland Italy.

The peninsula's main town, Cábras, lies languidly on the eastern side of its eponymous lagoon – Stagno di Cábras – which separates the Sínis from the rest of Sardinia. This huge lagoon covers 2,000ha and is one of Europe's most fascinating ecological wetlands. This sleepy fishing town's greatest claim to fame is as the headquarters of Sardinia's mullet fishing. The local delicacy, *bottarga*, or mullet roe, is nicknamed 'Sardinian caviar'. Fish *aficionados* will be spoilt for choice here at the many restaurants specializing in fishy delights.

For the only sight of note in Cábras, head to the southwest entrance to town on the banks of the lagoon and the Museo Cívico. This small museum showcases finds from Thárros such as urns from the tophet (children's burial ground), containing the bones of animals and children from the 7th to 2nd centuries BC. It also displays discoveries of the late 1990s from Cuccuru S'Arrius, about 4km south of Cábras. There are also pre-Nuraghic and Nuraghic artefacts excavated from the Sínis Peninsula. Take a look, too, at the display of *fassoni* and the ecology and flora of the area.

INFORMATION

- ⊞ C1
- ✉ 18km west of Oristano
- 🚌 Bus from Oristano
- ↔ Cúglieri (➤ 54), Monte Ferru (➤ 61), Oristano (➤ 40), San Salvatore (➤ 56), Thárros (➤ 45)

Museo Cívico Cábras

- ✉ Via Thárros, Cábras
- ☎ 0783 290636
- ◉ Jun–Sep daily 9–1, 4–8; Oct–May Tue–Sun 9–1, 3–7
- 🎫 Moderate (includes admission to Thárros)

Great swathes of flower meadows cover the Sínis Peninsula

43

Spiaggia della Pelosa

INFORMATION

➕ A1

✉ Capo Falcone, Stintino, 49km northwest of Sássari

🍴 Bars and restaurants on the beach (€–€€€)

🚌 Regular bus from Sássari in summer (1 hour 10 mins)

⛴ Authorised trips to Ísola Asinara from Stintino

❓ The car park at the beach is very expensive

Quite simply, this is one of the island's most beautiful beaches, an idyllic sweep of fine sand and exceptionally clear water.

It lies 2km north of Stintino – the northwestern point of Sardinia. Flour-fine white sand is lapped by crystalline shallow water in every shade of turquoise and hue of electric blue. It is guarded by a Spanish watchtower, Torre Falcone, on its own little islet on the northern side. To the north-east there are gorgeous views across to the islands of Asinara (Donkey Island) and Piana. The fine, soft sand with soft dune formations contrasts perfectly with the dark rocks of the Capo Falcone peninsula at the back of the beach. And the colour of the sea truly has to be seen to be believed. The only drawback is that the beach is extremely popular and quickly becomes very crowded in high season.

The Ísola Asinara lies across the sparkling waters, which is now a national park. Its chequered history includes use as a maximum security penal centre until the 1970s and a cholera quarantine station. The Romans called it Herculis Insula (Hercules' Island) and from late medieval times it was inhabited by shepherds and their flocks and by Ligurian tuna fishermen. Today it takes its name from the island's unique population of miniature albino donkeys. They, along with pigs and mouflons – wild sheep – are the only inhabitants on 16km-long 'Donkey Island'. The white sandy beaches are beautiful, the sea cobalt blue and shallow – and they are not crowded as the Parco Nazionale regulates access.

Clear as mineral water – the sea at Pelosa beach

Thárros

This is one of the island's top architectural sites on a promontory at the end of the Sínis Peninsula, guarded by a Spanish watchtower.

Evidence of human habitation in this area dates back to the 6th millennium BC before the Nuraghic civilization began to spread. By the 9th century BC the first Phoenician merchants landed at Thárros, the ancestor of Oristano. Later Thárros was abandoned, to escape the increasingly frequent raids by the Moors. As the local expression goes, '*Portant de Tharros sa perda a carros*' – 'they're bringing cartloads of stones from Thárros'. The stones were used to build the new town, originally named 'Aristanis' meaning 'between the ponds'.

It wasn't until 1956 that excavations began in earnest to reveal this prosperous Phoenician port. You can only see it properly once you enter the archaeological site as the ruins slope away onto the seaward side. Although most of what is now visible belongs to the Roman period, there are still remnants of the Phoenician city in a temple with Doric half-columns and, north of the main site, a tophet – or children's burial ground.

The Roman city had the usual shops, taverns, baths and amphitheatre. At the northern end you will find a relatively modest 2nd to 3rd-century AD amphitheatre, partially occupying the area of the tophet. Gladiatorial and wild beast contests were staged here for up to 8,000 people during the Roman era. Nowadays, there are open-air performances on a makeshift stage by the sea in high season. Sunset at Thárros is a magical experience.

INFORMATION

✚ C1
✉ 20km west of Oristano
☎ 0783 370019
🕐 Daily 9–6.30 (till dusk in high season). Outdoor performances begin 9.30pm
🚌 Regular buses from Oristano in summer (30 minutes)
♿ Difficult
🎫 Moderate (includes Museo Civico in Cábras)
🔁 Cúglieri (► 54), Monte Ferru (► 61), Oristano (► 40), San Salvatore (► 56), Sínis Peninsula (► 43)

The deep blue of the sea is a perfect backdrop to the evocative ruins

Tiscali

INFORMATION

➕ B3

✉ 20km southeast of Núoro

🕐 May–Sep daily 9–7;
Oct–Apr 9–5

💶 Moderate

♿ Not suitable – a stiff walk
is the only means of
access

↔ Cala Gonone (➤ 51),
Dorgali (➤ 54, 59), Gola
Su Gorruppu (➤ 61),
Golfo di Orosei (➤ 30),
Núoro (➤ 55)

❓ Guided tours can be
arranged through tourist
office in Oliena (Via
Grazia Deledda) ☎ 0784
286078 🕐 Jun–Aug
Mon–Sat 9–1, 4–7, Sun
9–1. Tours usually take a
whole day, departing
from Dorgali

A Nuraghic village concealed in a remote mountain chasm is one of Sardinia's most mysterious and atmospheric sights.

Renato Soru, president of Sardinia and the founder of the Italian internet service provider Tiscali, named his company after a huge silent cave on the top of a mountain in the centre of his native Sardinia, in which ancient islanders used to hide from their enemies. The company's inaugural advertising slogan was: 'Tiscali. From a land of silence comes a new way of communication'. In the heart of the wild Supramonte, Tiscali contains the remains of a village dating all the way back to the final Nuraghic period.

Monte Tiscali stands at 515m and within it is a wide crater concealing the Nuraghic village – originally a site of more than 60 round dwellings, most of them now ruined. It is thought that it was built in late Nuraghic times to escape the Roman domination; this was a perfect spot, given the rugged terrain and high crater walls. The site continued to be inhabited into medieval times, but was only discovered in the 19th century and is still under excavation. It is a very atmospheric spot, buried in the mountain with stalactites and trees growing inside and remnants of the *nuraghi* within.

It's best to take a guide to do this full-day trek (around 5 hours there and back), organised through the tourist information office in Oliena (see panel for details). However, should you wish to undertake it on your own, the best starting point is from the natural spring at Sorgente Su Gologone, next to the Hotel Su Gologone, just off the Oliena–Dorgali road (7km east of Oliena). Make sure you let someone know where you're going, wear sturdy shoes and adequate sun protection and take refreshments (especially water).

Valle dei Nuraghi

This valley of mysterious megalithic remains includes Nuraghe Santu Ántine – one of the island's greatest prehistoric monuments.

Like a castle dominating the plain set against a backdrop of extinct conical volcanoes, this *nuraghe*, dating from 1600BC, was once known as Sa Domu de Su Rei – the Royal Palace. The main tower probably reached to 21m before the top stones were removed in the 19th century for the village well in Torralba. It still is over 17m high and is constructed of 28 courses of stone blocks, held together without any mortar. The vast basalt blocks are 1.2m wide and 1.8m long. Staircases and corridors link the three-storey tower and in front is a magnificent courtyard with a well 20m deep. Seven corridors feed off from the courtyard among which is the *Cammino di Ronda Inferiore* (lower sentry walkway), carved out of the walls. From the top, now open to the elements and railed off, ruins of other *nuraghi* are visible dotted around the fields.

In Torralba, the Museo Archeológico showcases excavated items from the Valle dei Nuraghi, including pottery from the 12th century BC, and Phoenician, Greek and Roman artefacts in the Sala Santu Ántine. There is also a scale model of the *nuraghe* and, on the first floor, the Sala Romana has Roman columns and coins and, in the garden, a display of milestones from the Cágliari to Ólbia road – the first Roman road on the island.

INFORMATION

⊞ B2

⊠ 34km south of Sássari

↔ Sássari (► 42)

Nuraghe Santu Ántine

🚌 Bus from Sássari to Torralba, then 1-hour walk

🕐 Apr–Oct daily 9–dusk; Nov–Mar 9–5

🍽 Café at entrance to Nuraghe Santu Ántine (€€)

🎫 Moderate (includes entry to museum in Torralba)

Museo Archeológico

⊠ Via Carlo Felice 142, Torralba

🕐 Apr–Oct daily 9–8; Nov–Mar 9–5

Corridor in Santu Ántine

Villasimíus

Framed by *macchia* and pines, the former fishing village of Villasimíus is now a popular resort almost unfairly endowed with lovely beaches nearby.

INFORMATION

➕ D3

✉ 49km southeast of Cágliari

🍴 Numerous bars and restaurants (€€)

🚌 Regular bus from Cágliari in summer

🚢 Boat trips to islands of Cávoli and Serpentara on schooner *Matilda* leave from Marina daily in season

♿ Good access

↔ Monte dei Sette Fratelli (► 61)

Museo Archeológico

✉ Via Frau

🕐 Mid-Jun to mid-Sep Tue–Fri 10–1, 9–midnight; mid-Sep to mid-Jun Tue–Thu 10–1, Fri–Sun 10–1, 5–7

💶 Moderate

Red fishing nets at the harbour

The busiest part of Villasimíus is along the main street, Via Umberto I, which widens out at the two main squares, Piazza Gramsci and Piazza Incani at the heart of town. Off Via Umberto I on Via Frau is the Museo Archeológico showcasing local finds from Phoenician and Roman settlements and a 'room of the Spanish wreckage' devoted to artefacts recovered from a 16th-century shipwreck.

Spiaggia Simius is the nearest beach, accessible 1.5km down the Via del Mare. It has fine, white sand lapped by azure-green shallow seas. From here there are magnificent views of the offshore islands of Cávoli and Serpentara. Towards the south, the beach joins the Spiaggia Porto Giunco–Notteri. This is another enchanting corner of Villasimíus, separating the sea from the lagoon of Notteri, which is frequently home to a host of pink flamingos. On the western side the Spiaggia del Riso is gloriously framed by an amphitheatre of hills and mountains, while the beach is reminiscent of white grains of rice, hence the name '*del riso*' (of rice). In fact they're miniscule grains of translucent quartz.

The headland of Capo Carbonara is the most southeasterly point of Sardinia, complete with old fortress and harbour, and is accessible by a good road from Villasimíus. From here the high coast road north to Costa Rei is extraordinarily scenic. The first of many glorious beaches lies about 14km from Villasimíus – the Spiaggia Cala Sinzias – accessed by a short dirt road off the main road. Costa Rei itself is 11km away with swathes of blonde fine sand and shimmering, turquoise-green shallow seas.

SARDINIA'S
best

Beaches

ARCIPÉLAGO DE LA MADDALENA

The best beaches on La Maddalena are Cala Maiore, Spiaggia Bassa Trinità and Stagno Torto on the western coast and Cala Lunga on the northeast. On Caprera there are the Due Mari beaches in the south and, on the east coast, Cala Brigantino and Cala Colticcio. The other five main islands are only reachable by boat.

ALGHERO

Alghero (➤ 24) is on the Riviera del Corallo, which is named after the deep red coral formations that lie on the seabed on the submerged walls of Capo Cáccia, where you find the Grotta di Nettuno (➤ 31). The best beaches are immediately to the north of Alghero, including the Lido di San Giovanni, about 3km long, with plenty of facilities and accessible by foot from the port along the Passeggiata Busquets. It stretches along the coast to Fertília. Just to the west of here is the locals' favourite beach, Spiaggia Le Bombarde, with its lovely golden-white sand, parking facilities, bars/café and children's play area.

🚆 B1 ✉ Alghero 🚌 Local AF bus from Alghero stops at the turn-off for Le Bombarde

ARCIPÉLAGO DE LA MADDALENA

The main island, La Maddalena (➤ 25), has easily accessible beaches by the panoramic road, with the best being on the northern coasts. Spiaggia Bassa Trinità on the west has fine, white sand, and on the northeast coast the golden sands of Cala

The Lido beach at Alghero

Spalmatore are protected by promontories of pink granite rocks. South of La Maddalena, Santo Stefano has lovely beaches, especially on the eastern side of the island at Spiaggia del Pesce, where boats tend to stop. To the west, Spargi is the third largest island of the archipelago. The best beach here is Cala Corsara in the south, with white sand and sea in every colour from turquoise to cobalt blue. The best-known island of all is Budelli, famous for its Spiaggia Rosa (Pink Beach). The beautiful pink colour is made by a mix of pink granite rock particles and marine animal shells. The area is protected by the Archipelago National Park and, at present, can only be admired from the sea. Also to the north are Ísola Razzoli and Ísola Santa Maria, separated by the very narrow Passo degli Asinelli. Covered in *macchia* and grape vines, Santa

Maria's Cala Santa Maria beach has fine, white sand lapped by shallow, blue seas.

🚩 A3 🚢 Ferry from Palau 40km northwest of Ólbia 🍴 Bars and restaurants in La Maddalena)€–€€; not on beaches) ♿ Limited

BÁIA SARDINIA

Báia Sardinia's main beach is the Cala Battistoni. It has fine, white sand and azure-green shallow seas. It is extremely popular in high season and is very good for families. There are plenty of facilities and easy access.

🚩 A3 ✉ 9km west of Porto Cervo 🍴 Bars and restaurants (€€–€€€) 🚌 Bus service from Ólbia to Porto Cervo and then onward (15 mins) to Báia Sardinia.

BOSA MARINA

About 2.3km south of Bosa by road is the sandy beach of Bosa Marina. Popular with families and windsurfers, it has a large beach with shallow water. There are plenty of bars, restaurants, shops and facilities. About 1.5km south along the promenade is Spiaggia Turas – a large beach of fine sand lapped by deep water. To the north of Bosa town is the lesser known Cala S'Abba Druche, one of the area's best small beaches. Access is by a dirt track off the coastal road to Alghero.

🚩 A3 ✉ 42km south of Alghero 🚌 FdS buses from Alghero to Bosa (€)

CALA GONONE & GOLFO DI OROSEI

Cala Gonone itself has three good small beaches, all within walking distance from the harbour: the Spiaggia Centrale, which the resort fronts, then just south Spiaggia Palmasera and 1km beyond that, Spiaggia Sos Dorroles, spectacularly backed by a parapet of orange-coloured limestone cliff. Other beautiful beaches in the Golfo di Orosei include Cala Fuili, Cala Cartoe and, especially, Cala Luna; all are within a few kilometres of the harbour. The easiest access is by boat and there are regular trips from the harbour that also include excursions to the Grotta del Bue Marino (▶ 30). It is possible to reach Cala Luna on foot by a fairly precipitous rough track of around 4km. The last descent is very stony and a bit of a scramble, but you can always return on one of the regular boats back to Cala Gonone port. These 'castaway' beaches have a bar/café in summer, but you need to take your own shade and towels.

🚩 B1 ✉ Cala Gonone is 40km east of Núoro 🍴 Many cafés and restaurants in Cala Gonone (€–€€€); limited facilities on 'castaway' beaches (€) 🚌 Shuttle buses from Dorgali 10km away (20 mins)

COSTA DEL SUD

Southwest of Cágliari, the coastal road along the Costa del Sud is one of the island's most scenic and has 20 of Sardinia's best beaches. Rated among the top five in Europe, the beaches at Báia Chia are beautiful, with soft white sand and dunes, partly flanked by lagoons rich in local flora and fauna and backed by juniper

ITALIANS ON HOLIDAY

All of Sardinia's beaches are open to everyone. And, while it may be absurd to suggest that anyone could ever tire of the land that gave us Verdi, Vesuvius and Versace, those mainland Italians who want a change of scenery for their summer breaks come to Sardinia in their droves. Yet, even in August, only the main town beaches get crowded. While many northern European visitors like the privacy and space of the quiet coves, Italians like to parade up and down on the more sociable town beaches, which consequently can get very, very crowded.

51

trees. Spiaggia Sa Colonia is one of the most glorious and overlooks the site of the ancient Phoenician-Punic city of Bithia. Between Chia and Pula, the Spiaggia di Santa Margherita has a long white stretch of sand and a backdrop of scented Mediterranean *macchia* and pine trees. Head down to Capo Spartivento and Capo Cala Cipolla (next to the Baia Chia), which is only accessible by foot, but its picturesque beach and cliffs make it well worth the effort. It also has seven reefs – a paradise for scuba divers.

🞠 D2 ✉ 50km southwest of Cágliari 🍴 Selection of bars, cafés and restaurants (€–€€€) 🚌 Regular buses from Cagliari to Pula (17km from Chia)

SANDAL OF GOD

Legend says that God created Sardinia by stepping on it with his sandal. 'Sandalyon' (sandal) was the ancient name given to it by the Greeks and Phoenicians.

COSTA VERDE

On the west of the island, south of Oristano and northwest of Cágliari, this untamed coastline has sand dunes, cliffs and fine beaches. Two of the best are

Spiaggia della Piscinas – a huge swathe of fine, yellow sand with dunes rising to 30m like a miniature desert. Access is difficult, involving a 9km dirt track off the SS126 from Árbus and then offroad driving for some 20 minutes. Easily accessible is the Spiaggia S Nicolò, immediately north of Buggerru. It has long golden sands, splendid dunes and clear waters and, depending on the wind, is a favourite for surfers.

The endless sand at the mouth of the Piscinas river, Costa Verde

🞠 C1 ✉ Spiaggia della Piscinas 65km south of Oristano; Buggerru 84km south of Oristano 🍴 Couple of beach bars in summer at Spiaggia della Piscinas (€) and several cafés at Spiaggia S Nicolò (€–€€)

GOLFO ARANCI

This resort is more family-oriented than the Costa Smeralda but has the same gorgeous, white sandy beaches with shallow, azure seas; conveniently, the nearest to the resort are indicated in order from one to five. The best of them is the third beach – La Terza Spiaggia – accessed by a short road from the main drag.

🞠 A3 ✉ 18km northeast of Ólbia 🍴 Bars and restaurants (€€) 🚌 Bus from Ólbia (30 mins) in summer 🚆 Train from Ólbia (25 mins)

POETTO

For sun, sand and relaxation, Poetto beach is the magnet for the local Cágliaritani and visitors alike. The 6km stretch of soft, white sand lapped by a clear, turquoise sea is beautifully framed by the mountains of the Sárrabus and Capo Carbonara. It is also backed by the lagoon of Molentargius, frequented by flamingos and many other wetland birds. Loungers and parasols are available for hire and there are plenty of watersports available. The beach bristles with bars, cafés and eateries. At the westernmost point of Poetto, Marina Piccola is the liveliest part of the beach. Protected by the Sella del Diávolo promontory, the picturesque yacht basin is a fashionable local meeting place and top sailing centre. In July and August there's a concert area and an open-air cinema.

➕ D2 ✉ 8km southeast of Cágliari 🍴 Numerous cafés, bars and restaurants (€–€€€) 🚌 PQ bus from Cágliari's Piazza Matteotti (15 mins) ♿ Good facilities including wheelchairs for entering the water

PORTO CERVO (COSTA SMERALDA)

The Pevero coastline that has made Sardinia so famous is dotted with numerous beaches and coves accessed by turning down rough track roads off the road leading to Porto Cervo. West of the Cala di Volpe Bay, Capriccioli and Romazzino beaches are worth the detour. The lovely Portu Li Coggi beach (also known as the Spiaggia del Principe, the Prince's Beach), has very poor signposting, but is really worth a little effort. From Porto Cervo, start at Cala di Volpe, then keep the famous hotel to the right while heading south for about 2.5km. Before Capriccioli take the junction for Romazzino on the left. Head north and near the resort (after 1.4km) take a right towards the sea and after about 300m downhill you come to a barrier preventing car access. Cross the small gate that begins a short mule track to the shore. The best way to explore the Costa Smeralda is in a boat – it's the best way of getting to all those hideaway coves and beaches.

➕ A3 ✉ Costa Smeralda, about 12km north of Ólbia 🍴 Many cafés and restaurants, especially on the Piazzetta (€€€) 🚌 Regular buses from Ólbia

SANTA TERESA DI GALLURA

The town beach, Spiaggia Rena Bianca, is attractive but gets very crowded in season. But this coast is well endowed with long, sandy beaches. One of the best is 8km east – Spiaggia La Marmorata, set in one of Gallura's most beautiful bays. The sand is fine and golden, the green-azure sea is shallow and there's easy access by car. Southwest of Santa Teresa is Spiaggia Rena Maiori, close to a large holiday village and also easily accessible. The golden, sandy beach is fringed by pines and sand dunes and, even in high season, is rarely crowded thanks to the fact that it is very large.

➕ A2 ✉ 61km northwest of Ólbia 🍴 Numerous bars and restaurants in Santa Teresa (€–€€) 🚌 Bus from Ólbia

SAN TEODORO

Spiaggia Isuledda, just to the south of San Teodoro, is one of the island's most beautiful white sandy beaches, with lovely views of the Ísola Tavolara. To the north of the town, Spiaggia La Cinta is a gorgeous 4km stretch of finest white sand. It is backed by the lagoon Stagno di S Teodoro – an important wetland environment, very rich in birdlife.

➕ B3 ✉ 29km southeast of Ólbia 🍴 Both beaches have bars and restaurants (€–€€) 🚌 Bus from Ólbia (40 mins) or Núoro (1hr)

NATURAL BEAUTY

Sardinia has the most beautiful coastline in the whole of Italy, and some of the world's most idyllic beaches. Kilometre after kilometre of blond sands dip into waters of dazzling shades of aquamarine and emerald green. Elsewhere, rugged cliffs plunge into the sea and tiny coves wait to be explored. Many of the unpolluted waters really are as blue and as clear as a swimming pool – and some of the sandy coves can be quite deserted.

Spiaggia Rena Bianca, Santa Teresa di Gallura's main beach – before the crowds arrive

53

Towns & Villages

BOSA

This charming little town is clustered around the banks of the River Temo, crossed by the Ponte Vecchio bridge. Made of reddish stone with terracotta roofs, the jumble of little houses seems to glow, looking out over the palm-fronted esplanade past the fishing boats to the old tanneries on the opposite bank. There is a castle standing sentinel over the town, a cathedral and a medieval quarter with a fascinating tangle of alleys. This ancient town was founded by the Carthaginians, then adopted by the Romans and remained very prosperous until the 16th century. Many of the houses have been lovingly restored and it is a perfect place to while away a few days. As well as its laid-back appeal, it has good restaurants and is famous for its golden Malvasia dessert wine. Bosa Marina, the seaside resort, lies 2.3km to the west.
🚩 B1 ✉ 45km south of Alghero 🍴 Many bars and restaurants (€€) 🚌 FdS bus from Alghero (55 mins)

CÚGLIERI

Halfway up the slopes of Monte Ferru (➤ 61), this important agricultural town is, along with Seneghe, the island's leading producer of high-quality olive oil. Cúglieri is known for its superbly sited basilica, from where there are sublime views of the coast, as far as the cliffs of Porto Conte near Alghero on a clear day. The surrounding area is full of oak and chestnut forests and has several *nuraghi*, including Nuraghe Losa (➤ 37), *domus de janas* and *tombe dei giganti*.
🚩 B1 ✉ 43km north of Oristano 🍴 Limited choice of bars and restaurants (€€) 🚌 Bus from Oristano (1hr 20 mins)

The silver dome of the 15th-century basilica of Santa Maria della Neve in Cúglieri is visible from miles around

DORGALI

Ideally placed for excursions inland and to the spectacular Golfo di Orosei, this bustling market town is also famous for its handicrafts. Wool, wood, cork, silver and gold items are all produced and nearby are the vineyards of Oliena that produce excellent Cannonau wine. There is a small archaeological museum with finds from the nearby Grotta di Ispinigoli. This famous cave, estimated to be 180 million years old, has Europe's tallest stalagmite, towering at 38m. From the entrance, 280 steps lead 60m down into the fairytale grotto. Nine streams flow through these subterranean surroundings where the temperature remains at a constant 16–17°C.

➕ B1 ✉ 32km east of Núoro 🍴 Good choice of bars and restaurants (€€) 🚌 Buses run from Núoro (1hr 10 mins)

FORDONGIÁNUS

The Roman spa town of Forum Trainus on the banks of the River Tirso was known for its thermal waters, and today you can still visit the first century AD bath complex. The town is also renowned for the distinctive local red trachyte stone, and a sculpture competition is held here every summer.

➕ C2 ✉ 28km east of Oristano 🍴 A few restaurants and bars (€–€€) 🚌 ARST bus from Oristano

NÚORO

This overgrown mountain village of granite is at the heartland of Sardinia's traditions and, although not especially aesthetically pleasing, gave birth to distinguished literary figures such as Grazia Deledda (➤ 9). It is also home to one of the island's best museums, the Museo della Vita e delle Tradizioni Sarde – often referred to simply as the 'Museo del Costume' (➤ 58). The old part of town in the northeast spreads around Piazza San Giovanni and Corso Garibaldi. On the northern fringes is the Museo Deleddiano, home of the writer Grazia Deledda. On Piazza Santa Maria della Neve is the neoclassical cathedral, completed in 1854, and notable more for its quantity than its quality. Inside, among the mainly 20th-century paintings, the *Disputa de Gesù Fra i Dottori (Jesus's Dispute in the Temple)* is a 17th-century canvas attributed to the Neapolitan studio of Luca Giordano. Behind the cathedral there are spectacular views out across the valley to Monte Ortobene.

➕ B3 ✉ 100km southwest of Ólbia 🍴 Many bars and restaurants (€€) 🚌 Regular bus from Ólbia airport (1hr 45 mins); more limited service from Alghero (2.5hr) 🚉 Station is 15-minute walk from the centre. Train service to Cágliari (3hr 30 mins)

ORGOSOLO

A painted rock depicting 'the greedy landowner of Orgosolo' greets you just outside the entrance to this town of murals. Over 150 of them adorn the streets and corners in a tradition dating back to 1975. Nowadays, many are devoted to modern-day as well as political themes – from folklore figures such as the *mamuthones* to the destruction of the

MAMOIADA

Every year at Carnival time this otherwise rather colourless town near Núoro erupts into a frenzy of shaggy sheepskinned-men wearing demonic black wooden masks and weighed down by heavy cowbells. These traditional costumed figures, known as *mamuthones*, have pagan origins, and this ritual is an attempt to drive out demons before the spring and the new arrival of fecundity. They represent defeated men and animals and are subjugated by the *issokadores* – men dressed in red and white wielding lassoos. As well as during Carnival, this scene is re-enacted on 17 January for the Festa di Sant'Antonio. By legend Sant'Antonio took hell's fire to give to man and for this festival bonfires are lit throughout the village. The Museo delle Maschere Mediterranee has an interesting exhibition of masks and mannequins.

Mural in Orgosolo

Twin Towers in New York on 11 September 2001 and the fall of Baghdad in 2003. There are, too, allusions to the sheep rustling and kidnappings for which this town was once notorious. Popularly known as the 'capital' of Barbágia, the region's most notorious bandits are said to have taken refuge here in the first half of the 20th century when the town averaged a murder every two months. Nowadays it's rather quieter, although the locals have adorned some street signs with bullet holes.

✚ B3 ✉ 20km south of Núoro 🍴 Bars and restaurants (€–€€) 🚌 Regular buses from Núoro (35 mins) ❓ The Festa dell'Assunta takes place in Orgosolo on 15 August – a highlight of Barbágia and one of the top colourful processions of the region

SAN SALVATORE

The church of San Salvatore opens in late August to celebrate his feast and pilgrims arrive to take up residence in the little houses, known as *cumbessias*. The climax is the re-enactment of the rescue of the statue of San Salvatore from Moorish attackers. Hundreds of young men in boxer shorts and white ruffled shirts make the 8km dash, barefoot, from Cábras to San Salvatore and back again the following day. The statue bounces perilously away on its palanquin and the locals' belief is that by pounding the ground barefoot the earth will be stirred and fertility restored. More pagan than religious, you would imagine, and you would be right. The church was erected on top of a former pagan sanctuary, constructed in Nuraghic times as a water temple and later dedicated to Venus and Mars.

SAN SALVATORE

On the Sínis Peninsula near the watery lagoon world, the dusty little village of San Salvatore looks like a film set. It has a bar, shuttered houses piled together, swirling dust and looks every bit set to stage the shoot-out from High Noon. It has been used as the setting for spaghetti westerns, but its great claim to fame these days is the Barefoot Race (Corsa degli Scalzi) when the village bursts into frenzied activity (see panel). The festival is centred around the sanctuary of San Salvatore – one of Sardinia's *chiese novenari* – churches open for only nine days a year.

✚ C1 ✉ 28km west of Oristano 🍴 One bar, Abraxas Chiosco Bar (di Pinna Vincenzo) at the entrance to the village ( )

TÉMPIO PAUSÁNIA

Témpio Pausánia, in the heart of the Gallura, is at 550m and surrounded by dense forests of cork oak. This granite hilltop town is a centre of cork manufacturing and wine production, especially Vermentino. Always a rival of Ólbia, it is now joint capital of the province of Ólbia-Témpio. It is a town of churches, the most important of which is the 15th-century Cattedrale di San Pietro, substantially rebuilt in the 19th century. Next door, the Oratorio del Rosario, built originally by the Aragonese but rebuilt in the 18th century, has an elaborate baroque altar decorated with pure gold.

✚ A2 ✉ 45km west of Ólbia 🍴 Good range of restaurants and bars

Shuttered houses in San Salvatore

(€–€€) 🚌 ARST buses from Ólbia (1.5hr) 🚂 *Trenino verde* in summer from Arzachena (www.treninoverde.com)

For Children

AQUADREAM WATER PARK

Go wild and wet on the chutes and slides in the Aquadream Water Park at Báia Sardinia.

🔲 A3 ✉ Báia Sardinia, 4.5km west of Porto Cervo ☎ 0789 99511
🕐 Mid-Jun to mid-Sep daily 10–6 🚌 Bus from Porto Cervo (15 mins)
✋ Expensive

GIARA DI GESTURI

This 45sq km plain is a favourite place for the wild *cavallini* (little horses) and red long-horned bulls that roam around here. It's also a favourite area for nature walks through *macchia* and cork oaks and beautiful springtime flowers, including several species of wild orchid. Nature walks last a couple of hours and the guide explains how to distinguish between edible and poisonous plants, which plants are used as local medicines and some of the archaeology of the area.

🔲 C2 ✉ 5km west of Barúmini 🚌 ARST buses link from Cágliari and Barúmini ❓ Organised educational excursions available such as walking visits, trekking, mountain biking or 4x4 rides. Contact Jara Escursioni 070 936 4277; www.parcodellagiara.it, or Sa Jara Manna, 070 938170; www.sajaramanna.it

PARCO SARDEGNA IN MINIATURA

Very close to Nuraghe Su Nuraxi is the Parco Sardegna in Miniatura – a miniature theme park of the whole island covering 30,000sq m. Highlights include model reconstructions of Cágliari, the beaches of the Costa Smeralda, Su Nuraxi and a reconstruction of a Nuraghic village. A new Native American Village opened in 2007.

🔲 C2 ✉ 1km west of Barúmini ☎ 070 936 1004; www.sardegnainminiatura.it 🕐 Apr–Sep daily 9–6; Oct–Mar Sat–Sun 9–6 🍴 Picnic area and restaurant ✋ Expensive (boat trips included, train trips extra)

TRENINO VERDE

This little green train with steam or diesel engine is a tourist service run by the Sardinian Railways in summer. It crosses the most interesting areas of the island that are otherwise difficult to reach. There are three narrow-gauge scenic routes – from Palau to Témpio (1 hr 30 mins) in the north, Bosa Marina to Macomér (1 hr 47 mins) in the centre and Árbatax to Mándas (5 hrs) in the east. This last line, connecting the coastal area of Árbatax with the inland, has been called 'the most beautiful line in the world' but its whole 160km length may test the patience of little ones. By car take the SS125 to Tortoli then the turning for Árbatax; by train, travel to Árbatax train station to join the *trenino verde*.

☎ 070 5793 0346; www.treninoverde.com 🕐 Mid-Jun to early Sep
✋ Expensive

CHILDREN WELCOME

Sardinians love children and go out of their way to make them welcome. Every kind of accommodation is on offer and staying on a farm in an *agriturismo* can be a great hit with little ones. Many of the resorts have hotels that have great facilities for children (such as Le Meridien Chia Laguna Village). Resorts such as Chia, Cala Gonone, Cannigione and Báia Sardinia are especially family-oriented. And pizza and glorious *gelato* (ice cream) are always great favourites.

Sardinian children are keen participants in the island's colourful festivals

Prehistoric Sites & Museums

NURAGHIC BUILDERS

Dating back to the mists of time, the *nuraghi* – conical stone dwellings – are found in every corner of the island. Built some 3,500 years ago, there are still remains of 7,000 of these mysterious structures created by people who left no written records. There is a Sard saying that translates as 'A modern builder guarantees his work for five years, but the Nuraghic builder guaranteed his for 5,000.' They may not have lasted quite that long yet, but Nuraghic craftsmanship has certainly stood the test of time.

MUSEO ARCHEOLÓGICO NAZIONALE, CÁGLIARI

Castello houses the most important artistic treasures of the city in the Citadella dei Musei – the highlight of which is the Museo Archeológico Nazionale. This is the island's most important collection of artefacts from prehistoric to Roman times. The museum's first level is devoted to the Pre-Nuraghic millennia, including obsidian tools and little fat, round fertility stone goddesses – part of the Great Mother Goddess cult – often found in *domus de janas* ('fairy houses'). But perhaps most fascinating are the *bronzetti* – bronze statuettes used as votive offerings, which depict anything from stags and shepherds to demonic figures. There are extraordinary displays of jewellery too, from necklaces made of fox teeth to an exquisite filigree gold necklace and earrings from the 4th century BC. Some explanatory panels are in English.

➕ D2 ⊠ Piazza dell'Arsenale ☎ 070 684000 ⊙ Apr–Oct Tue–Sun 9–8; Nov–Mar 9–12, 2–8 💰 Moderate

MUSEO NAZIONALE SANNA, SÁSSARI

After the Museo Archeológico in Cágliari, this is the island's most significant collection of archaeological finds. It is named after Giovanni Sanna, a mining engineer, and was built to house his art collection of mostly 18th-century paintings. Treasures in the museum include prehistoric finds from 2700BC, but the greatest attractions are from the Nuraghic era. There is a fine array of bronze statuettes, many from the Valle dei Nuraghi, and displays from *domus de janas* and artefacts from Phoenician, Carthaginian and Roman eras.

➕ B1 ⊠ Via Roma 64 ☎ 079 272203 ⊙ Tue–Sun 9–8 💰 Inexpensive

MUSEO DELLA VITA E DELLE TRADIZIONI SARDE, NÚORO

Often referred to simply as the 'Museo del Costume', this is the island's best museum of Sard life and costumes. The collection of 7,000 items may seem daunting, but it is easy to cherry-pick what interests most in this Sardinian village-like setting. There are superb costumes and insights into wedding ceremonies and pre-nuptial gifts such as the *isprugadente*, one end of which was for cleaning ears and the other for teeth. Gorgeous jewellery – for both men and women – includes everything from intricately crafted silver filigree to wild boar tusks and sharks' teeth. Equally fascinating is the display of breads – over 600 varieties – and sweetmeats linked with annual festivities. The highlight is the display of spooky masks and hairy costumes from the Barbágia still used in carnival and feast-day processions.

🚌 B3 ✉ Via A Mereu 56 ☎ 0784 257035 ⏰ Mid-Jun to Sep daily 9–8; Oct to mid-Jun 9–1, 3–7

NECROPOLI DI ANGHELU RUJU

This necropolis of 38 prehistoric rock-cut tombs is one of Sardinia's most important *domus de janas* burial grounds. Dating back to between 3300 and 2700BC, some of the chambers have wall inscriptions at the entrance and sculpted bull's horns. Bronze Age artefacts excavated here in 1905 are on display in the Museo Archeológico in Cágliari (► 58).

🚌 B1 ✉ 7km north of Alghero ⏰ Apr–Oct daily 9–7; Nov–Mar daily 9.30–4 💶 Moderate

NURAGHE DI PALMAVERA

This prehistoric village consisted of about 50 houses grouped around the ruined central palace-tower, dating from the 14th and 13th centuries BC. There is also a circular Capanna delle Riunioni, or meeting hut, with a low stone bench running round the walls, thought to have been used for meetings or religious gatherings. At the centre is a plaster copy of the orginal stool which is on display in Sássari's Museo Nazionale Sanna (► 58).

🚌 B1 ✉ 10km west of Alghero ⏰ Apr–Oct daily 9–7; Nov–Mar daily 9.30–4 💶 Moderate

S'ENA' E THOMES

Near to Serra Orios (► below) is this *tomba dei giganti*. A walk of about 200m from the road brings you to this good example of a mass grave, dominated by a central standing stone that closed off the burial chamber.

🚌 B3 ✉ 3km north of crossroads with Núoro–Orosei road 💶 Free

SERRA ORIOS, DORGALI

Set among wild olive groves, this prehistoric village of *nuraghi* is very atmospheric. There are remains of what may have been temples, and about 70 houses clustered around courtyards and alleys leading to the communal wells. Built from huge basalt megaliths, the temples Tempietto A and B are thought to have been for visiting pilgrims and the villagers respectively. The village was probably occupied from 1500 to 250BC.

🚌 B3 ✉ 11km northwest of Dorgali ⏰ Hourly visits daily 9–1, 4–7 (till 5 in winter), in Italian only 🍴 Café on site 💶 Moderate

GIANTS' TOMBS

The Nuraghic graves are known as *tombe dei giganti* (giants' tombs). This Sardinian development of the dolmen includes a long burial chamber and a semicircular space for ceremonies called the *esedra*. Marked by standing stones, at the centre of the *esedra* is a single monolithic slab hewn from granite, often 4m high – a majestic door representing the entrance to the afterlife. These superhuman dimensions do indeed suggest the work of giants, but in reality they were probably used and reused by all members of the tribe.

Standing stones mark the 'giant's tomb' at Li Lolghi, Arzachena (above)

Entrance to the Museo Nazionale Sanna in Sássari (opposite top)

One of the costumes on display in Núoro's Museo della Vita e delle Tradizioni Sarde (opposite bottom)

Wild Places

Dramatic granite mountains in the Valle della Luna, Gallura

GALLURA

Jagged granite mountains line Gallura's shore, while the region's loftiest mountain, Monte Limbara (1,359m), is cloaked in pine forest. Inland, this is also the region of the cork oak forests with their distinctive reddish bark, which is used to make corks for most of Italy's wine bottles. Northwest of Témpio Pausánia, the Valle della Luna (Valley of the Moon) is a fantastic landscape.

✚ A2 ✉ 56km west of Olbia

ÍSOLA ASINARA

'Donkey Island' became a national park in 1997, after a colourful history including use as a prison and a quarantine centre for cholera victims. It takes its name from its population of albino donkeys, who, along with pigs and wild sheep (mouflon) are the only inhabitants. The sea is cobalt blue and the sandy beaches are glorious – and uncrowded, as access is only possible by authorised excursion from Stintino. You need to bring your own refreshments, as there is nothing available on the island.

✚ A1 ✉ Off the northwest tip of Sardinia 🚢 Excursions from Stintino Easter–Sep

ÍSOLA DEI CÁVOLI AND ÍSOLA SERPENTARA

These two islands lie off Capo Carbonara, the southeasternmost point of Sardinia, and are part of the Capo Carbonara protected marine area. Ísola dei Cávoli derives its name, rather unromantically, from cabbages (there are cabbage plants on the island) and Ísola Serpentara from its sinuous shape, but both islands are granite covered with scented *macchia* and seabirds, and have a rocky coastline punctuated by pristine beaches.

✚ D3 ✉ Off Capo Carbonara 🚢 Excursions from Marina di Villasimíus in summer

MONTE FERRU

North of Oristano, the SS292 winds up to the rugged triangle of Monte Ferru (Iron Mountain). There are eight communes that comprise the Communità Montana, all characterised by the surrounding densely forested highland studded with gnarled cork oaks, where mouflon and deer roam. The highest peak is 1,050m. The huge red ox (*bue rosso*) grazes the pastures here, prized for its strength – seen pulling the carriage of Sant'Efisio during the festival – and for its meat.
➕ B1 ✉ 27km north of Oristano

MONTE DEI SETTE FRATELLI

The mountains of Sette Fratelli (Seven Brothers) are a natural oasis covered in rich forestland with rugged peaks that rise above 1,000m. This wild corner of Sardinia is known as the Sárrabus and is inhabited by some of the island's last remaining deer (*cervo sardo*), who take cover under the mantle of fragrant *macchia*, cork and holm oak. It is also rich in wild boar, hare, partridge and birdlife. To get here, the winding and very scenic SS125 east of Cágliari goes north of the Monte dei Sette Fratelli; there are maps available at the Caserma Forestale Campu Omu (Forestry Corps station), opposite the turn-off to Burcei, showing the walks in the area. To the northwest of Villasimíus, off the SP17 to Castiádas there is a very good access point for the Monte dei Sette Fratelli and the Cooperativa Monte dei Sette Fratelli here has a huge array of excursions on offer.
➕ D3 ✉ 52km northeast of Cágliari

GOLA SU GORRUPPU

This is one of Europe's most spectacular gorges, carved out of limestone by the River Flumineddu, with limestone cliffs soaring to more than 400m. The gorge is 8km long, and you need proper equipment and a guide to venture very far inside.
➕ B3 ✉ 10km south of Dorgali

In the Monte dei Sette Fratelli you may come across wild pigs (below left) and dramatic rocky outcrops (below right)

Places to Have Lunch

FISH AND SEAFOOD

Although by tradition Sardinians are '*pastori, non pescatori*' (shepherds, not fishermen), fish and seafood are now widely available, certainly in all the coastal regions. *Spigole* (sea bass), *orate* (gilthead) and *tonno* (tuna) are all delicious grilled or barbecued. *Aragosta* (lobster) is another great favourite, especially around Alghero, as well as *calamari* (squid), *polpi* (octopus) and many other seafoods.

*Via Roma in Cágliari
is lined with cafés*

CAFÉ DEL PORTO (€–€€)

The only café/bar at Villasimíus's marina and port is a good place for a snack and admiring the views.
✉ Porto di Villasimíus, Villasimíus ☎ 070 797 8036 🕐 Daily 7am–2am

COCO LOCO CAFÉ (€)

This is a lovely spot to enjoy a long cool drink or a *gelato*. Good salads and snacks are also served on the pine- and palm-fronted seafront terrace.
✉ Piazza della Torre 13, Marina di Torre Grande ☎ 079 268023 🕐 Daily 7.30am–3am

LE DUNE (€)

Have lunch in the dunes in this alfresco bar/café, within a stone's throw of the beach. Relax in the colonial-style wickerwork chairs on the sand or seek out the cool shade under the veranda.
✉ Le Meridien Chia Laguna, Chia ☎ 070 92391 🕐 Drinks and pizzeria daily in season 12.30–3, snack bar 3–6

IL GHIOTTO (DI ROBERTO PEANA) (€)

This 'snackeria' specialises in *prodotti tipici* – cold cuts of meat and salami, cheeses, pizza, salads and sandwiches served in a buffet lunch. If you don't fancy a full meal, have an *aperitivo* and enjoy a free tasting of the various goodies. There's also a shop with tempting displays of Sardinian specialities.
✉ Piazza Civica 23, Alghero ☎ 079 974820 🕐 Daily in season 12.30–3.30

HOTEL/RESTAURANT ISPINIGOLI (€–€€)

Very conveniently located for the Grotto, the panoramic restaurant terrace is a good place to relax while waiting for a tour of the Grotto, which departs on the hour. All tastes are catered for with set menus for vegetarians, fish/seafood or traditional meat options and menus especially for children.
✉ Below entrance to the Grotto, Grotta Ispinigoli ☎ 0784 95268; www.hotelispinigoli.com

RISTORANTE AL PORTO (€€)

Here you can feast on local delicacies in the locals' favourite restaurant, overlooking the port.
✉ Via Marco Polo 2, Cala Gonone ☎ 078 493 185; www.hotelpop.com

SARDINIA
where to...

Cágliari and the South

PRICES

Approximate prices for a three-course meal for one, excluding drinks and wine:

€ = under €26
€€ = €26–€55
€€€ = over €55

TRADITIONAL CUISINE

Meat forms the basis of traditional Sardinian cuisine – *la cucina tipica Sarda*. Lamb, beef, kid goat and wild boar are all favourites, spit-roasted or grilled and smothered with fragant herbs. A real speciality is suckling pig (*porceddu* or *porcetto*), which you usually need to order the day before in restaurants. That allows time to massage the skin of the piglet in herbs and olive oil before swaddling it in sea salt. It is then slow-roasted over an open fire while being basted to golden, crispy perfection.

BARÚMINI

SA LOLLA ALBERGO RISTORANTE (€€)
Set in an old, restored country house, this restaurant has magnificent views over the Giara landscape. The rustic atmosphere and setting is complemented by the excellent Sardinian and Italian dishes.
✉ Via Cavour 49 ☎ 070 936 8419 🕐 Thu–Mon

BUGGERRU

PIZZERIA SAN NICOLÒ (€–€€)
A restaurant with stunning views over sweeping stretches of white sand often buffeted with big surf. Fresh fish and seafood, such as locally caught sea bass and tuna, top the menu.
✉ Località San Nicolo ☎ 0781 54359; www.ristorantesannicolo.it 🕐 Daily

CÁGLIARI

S'APPOSENTU AL TEATRO LIRICO (€€–€€€)
Opposite the T Hotel, this new theatre restaurant is already very popular. Under the watchful eye of chef Roberto Petza, the cuisine is beautifully presented modern Sardinian with the emphasis on fishy delights. You must reserve ahead.
✉ Via Sant' Alenixedda ☎ 070 408 2315 🕐 Mon–Sat

DAL CORSARO (€€€)
This is a family-run temple to gastronomy in elegant surroundings. It is an institution of the Cágliari culinary scene, attracting gourmets and fashionistas. Service is exemplary and the wine list is long, reflecting the depth of pockets needed here.
✉ Piazzale Regina Margherita 28 ☎ 070 664318 🕐 Mon–Sat; closed 2 weeks mid-Aug

RISTORANTE FLORA (€€€)
This well-known restaurant specialises in very good seasonal dishes in a refined atmosphere. Expect all the trappings of a grand *salotto*, complete with marble and service that is superb.
✉ Via Sássari 45 ☎ 070 664735 🕐 Mon–Sat; closed Aug

RISTORANTE MARIÒ (€€)
The intimate atmosphere and Sardinian food specialities are most welcoming. Home-made pasta such as *spaghetti alla spada* (swordfish) and lasagne with aubergines are excellent. Try to leave room for the sublime warm chocolate pudding.
✉ Via Genovesi 16 (easily accessible by the lift from the Bastione) ☎ 0706 53564; www.decandia.esiti.net 🕐 Mon–Sat; closed Mon lunch

SPINNAKER (€€€)
The first-floor terrace restaurant has glorious views of the Golfo degli Ángeli. The speciality is fresh fish and seafood, though there is a very good pizzeria downstairs.

✉ Località Marina Piccola, Poetto Beach ☎ 070 370295
🕐 May–Sep Tue–Sun

ÍSOLA DI SAN PIETRO

DA NICOLÒ (€€€)

This famous restaurant has a faithful following. Dine alfresco on the palm-shaded terrace, where fish specialities include traditional Theabarkina dishes (a local blend of Ligurian, Mediterranean, and North African cuisines) like *cashca'*, couscous, tuna *bottarga* (roe) and salt-cured tuna fillet.
✉ Corso Cavour 32
☎ 0781 854048
🕐 Easter–Sep Tue–Sun

AL TONNO DI CORSA (€€€)

Just a few minutes from the seafront in the historic area of the upper town, this restaurant has all kinds of tuna and fish specialities. It also does excellent pasta and Mediterranean dishes, served on outdoor terraces – or rooms indoors. An open kitchen gives a bird's-eye view of how your dish is progressing.
✉ Via Marconi 47 ☎ 0781 855106 🕐 Tue–Sun (open Mon in Jul and Aug); closed 7 Jan–end Feb

NORA

HOTEL BAIA DI NORA (€€)

At this pleasant alfresco restaurant set in lush gardens, you can feast on light dishes such as seafood salad. Try perhaps too the *affogato al caffè* – vanilla ice cream with hot espresso coffee.
✉ Località Su Guventeddu
☎ 070 924 5551;
www.hotelbaiadinora.com
🕐 Easter–Oct daily

VILLASIMÍUS

RISTORANTE CARBONARA (€€)

This traditional restaurant makes up for its rather lacklustre interior with large portions and good fish. Choose your delicacy from the platter of fresh offerings and don't be surprised to see lobster antennae waving at you.
✉ Via Umberto I, 60 ☎ 070 791270 🕐 Thu–Tue 12.30–2.30, 8–11

I GINEPRI (€€–€€€)

The Sofitel Timi Ama's beachside restaurant serves light lunches and traditional Sardinian cuisine in the evening and delicious fish dishes. The *tagliatelle ai frutti del mare* is especially good.
✉ Sofitel Thalassa Timi Ama, Località Notteri ☎ 070 79791; www.sofitel.com

STELLA MARIS HOTEL (€€)

There are two elegant sea-facing dining rooms with luxurious interiors, one inside and one outside. The restaurant with veranda outside has an especially lovely location with the sound of the water lapping and rustling of the pine trees. Fish is the speciality here.
✉ Località Campulongu
☎ 070 797100; fax 070 797367; www.stella-maris.com

OFFAL DELICACIES

You will see offerings on the menu that are not to everyone's taste, even to the most stoic of carnivores. Horse and donkey meat appear alongside offal delicacies such as *sa córdula* (roasted or barbecued sheep's entrails), *sanguinaccio* (black pudding made with pig's blood), *cordula* (lamb tripe stewed, grilled or fried) or *li pedi di agnoni* (lamb's feet).

65

Oristano and the West

FINE WINES

Sardinian wines are among the finest in the world, but as they are so sought after and produced in relatively small quantities, vintages often run out after a few months. The best reds mainly come from the local Cannonau grape; for whites look out for Vermentino and Vernaccia. Some of the wines are made by the traditional method of leaving the grapes to ferment for up to four weeks, producing a chemical reaction that has been claimed to stave off heart disease. The inhabitants of the Núoro province (famous for its Cannonau wine) have an extremely high life expectancy: their number of centenarians is an amazing three times the Western average.

CÁBRAS

IL CAMINETTO (€€)
This popular restaurant specialises in fish and seafood. Mullet features widely: as *bottarga*, and in delicacies such as *sa merca* (salted mullet cooked in herbs) or *mrecca* (boiled mullet in pond grass).
✉ Via Cesare Battisti 8
☎ 0783 391139 ◷ Tue–Sun

SA FUNTÀ (€€)
A real taste of Sardinia, complete with its own Nuraghic well. The specialities, too, are authentically Sardinian, many based on old recipes. Fishy delights include *burrida* (marinated dogfish), *anguilla con carciofi* (eel with artichokes) and *seppiette alla vernaccia* (cuttlefish with white wine).
✉ Via Garibaldi 25 ☎ 0783
290685 ◷ Mon–Sat; closed mid-Dec to Feb

MARINA DI TORRE GRANDE

MAESTRALE (€€)
On the seafront with a lovely terrace, this restaurant is deservedly popular. The speciality is fresh fish and seafood.
✉ Lungomare Torregrande
☎ 0783 22121 ◷ Tue–Sun

ORISTANO

COCCO & DESSÌ (€€)
Innovative cuisine is on offer in this fashionable restaurant that's also a bit quirky – the choice of dining spaces includes a gazebo. The menu changes to reflect seasonal specialities. Pizzas are available in the evening.
✉ Via Tirso 31 ☎ 0783
300720 ◷ Tue–Sun; closed Sun eve and 3 weeks in Jan

CRAF (€€)
The vaulted dining room was once a 17th-century granary and is atmospheric and welcoming. The seasonal menu is varied and has tasty offerings for both meat and fish eaters. Soups, such as *panne frattau*, made of hearty Sardinian bread, are a meal in themselves. Horse and donkey also feature.
✉ Via de Castro 34 ☎ 078
370669 ◷ Mon–Sat

IL FARO (€€–€€€)
This is a class act, offering traditional Sardinian specialities in an elegant yet relaxed restaurant. Seasonal dishes predominate and there is a good wine list with emphasis on local wines.
✉ Via Bellini 25 ☎ 0783
70002 ◷ Mon–Sat; closed third week of Dec to third week of Jan

SENEGHE

IL BUE ROSSO (€€)
The Red Ox occupies a former 1920s dairy, with lovely views of the surrounding hills. It specialises in the local *bue rosso* beef, prized by gourmets, but other local delicacies on the menu include *casiz olu* (cow's cheese). The restaurant is part of the Slow Food Movement, so is perfect for a leisurely meal.
✉ Piazzale Montiferru 3/4
☎ 0783 54384 ◷ Tue–Sun

Núoro and the East

CALA GONONE

RISTORANTE AL PORTO (€€)

Here you can feast on local delicacies in the locals' favourite restaurant overlooking the port. Host Simone Spanu is infectious in his enthusiasm for seafood – fishermen call him as they approach the dock to advise him of the catch of the day. Swordfish, octopus, succulent king prawns and enormous lobsters all feature regularly, along with 'Sardinian caviar' (*bottarga*), served here to perfection. There are also meat-based dishes.

✉ Hotel Pop, Via Marco Polo 2 ☎ 078 493185

DORGALI

RISTORANTE ALBERGO SANT'ELENE (€€)

From the terrace of this hillside restaurant there are glorious views and the typical regional cuisine is no less splendid. Roast suckling pig, lamb, sea bass and appetizers of home-made paté are complemented by the good wine and friendly service.

✉ Località Sant'Elene (3km off the SS125 from Dorgali) ☎ 0784 94572 🕐 Tue–Sun (open Mon in summer); closed Jan

COLIBRÌ (€€)

This warm and welcoming family-run restaurant specialises in traditional Sardinian cuisine such as *cinghiale* (wild boar) and *porcetto* (suckling pig). It also serves up very good fish dishes.

✉ Via Gramsci 14 (corner of Via Floris) ☎ 0784 96054 🕐 Mon–Sat (open Sun Jul–Aug)

NÚORO

IL RIFUGIO (€–€€)

Close to Madonna delle Grazie, this bustling trattoria/pizzeria is very popular with the locals. Home-made pasta and pizza are specialities and the pizza makers (*pizzaioli*) are an entertainment in themselves.

✉ Via Antonio Mereu 28/36 ☎ 0784 232355 🕐 Thu–Tue

OLIENA

SU GOLOGONE (€€€)

This very good restaurant is extremely popular. The Sardinian cuisine is based on recipes handed down through the generations, and includes delicious antipasti and home-made pasta as well as the speciality *porceddu* (suckling pig).

✉ Hotel Su Gologone, Località Su Gologone ☎ 0784 287512; www.sugologone.it

ORGOSOLO

RESTAURANT/HOTEL AI MONTI DEL GENNARGENTU (€€)

Lying 5km from Orgosolo, this pleasant rustic restaurant is well placed for discovering the local mountain sights. The restaurant specialises in traditional mountain food, based on Sardinian meats.

✉ Località Settiles ☎ 0784 402374

OLDEST GRAPES

Desiccated grapes, recently found in several Sardinian locations, have been DNA tested and proved to be the oldest grapes in the world, dating back to 1200BC. The Cannonau wine is made with the same variety of grape so may qualify as the mother of all European wines. Very good dessert wines include Moscato and Malvasia – a delicious golden wine for which Bosa is especially famous. *Mirto* (pronounced 'meer-toe') is a potent liqueur made from the Sardinian myrtle berry, deliciously redolent of lavender and blueberry.

Sássari and the Northwest

FIREWATER

The island's legendary firewater, distilled from the winemaking leftovers, rather like grappa, is known as *su fil'e ferru* – 'rod of iron'. Locals say that it's named after the practice of sticking a piece of wire in the soil to mark its hiding place. But, at around 40 per cent proof, it could also have something to do with its head-splitting strength.

ALGHERO

ANGEDRAS RESTAURANT (€€)

Chef Alessandro Tesi prepares a short, well-chosen menu of seafood tasting plates (*degustazione di mare*), home-made pasta such as *spaghetti alla chitarra con vongole e fiori du zucca* (hand-made spaghetti with clams and courgette flowers), fresh fish and seafood and meat-based dishes. Traditional Sardinian puddings are delicious. Outdoor seating is available overlooking the port and sunset.

✉ Via Cavour 31, corner of Bastioni Marco Polo ☎ 079 073 5078

BELLA NAPOLI (€–€€)

Neapolitan owned pizzeria with generous portions and good pasta dishes as well as pizzas. Good pasta dishes include *ravioli di ricotta*, with ricotta cheese, and *penne alla Siciliana*, spicy quill-shaped pasta.

✉ Piazza Civica 29 ☎ 079 983014 ⏰ Thu–Tue

CAFÉ LATINO (€–€€)

Overlooking the port, this is the perfect spot to chill out under the white parasols or inside among the cool stone vaults. Good snacks incude *panini*, pizzas and delicious ice-creams. Or enjoy a long cool beer or cocktail while watching the boats and the world go by.

✉ Bastioni Magellano 10 ☎ 079 976541 ⏰ Jul–Aug daily 9am–11pm; Sep–Jun Wed–Mon 9am–11pm

TRATTORIA AL REFETTORIO (€€)

Chic and atmospheric wine bar off Via Roma with excellent nibbles to accompany your *aperitivo*. The restaurant food is also good – and there is outside, covered seating. Fresh fish and seafood as well as dishes such as wild boar and other carnivorous delights fill the menu.

✉ Carreró del Porxo (Vicolo Adami) 47 ☎ 079 973 1126; www.alrefettorio.it ⏰ Wed–Mon

BOSA

BORGO SANT'IGNAZIO (€€)

Atmospheric bistro in the alleys of the old town where specialities include local *aragosta* (lobster), as well as Sardinian meat specialities. Being on the *strada della malvasia di Bosa*, it also has a good selection of Malvasia dessert wines to accompany your pudding.

✉ Via Sant'Ignazio 33 ☎ 0785 374662 ⏰ Tue–Sun 1–3, 7.30–11 (reduced hours out of season)

SA PISCHEDDA (€€)

This excellent restaurant is part of the Slow Food Movement. Linger over seasonal delicacies and enjoy a glass of Malvasia wine with your dessert. Its sister restaurant is the Ponte Vecchio, on a jetty above the river, which specialises in seafood in a very romantic setting (summer only).

✉ Via Roma 8 ☎ 0785 373065 ⏰ Apr–Sep daily; Oct–Mar Wed–Mon

CASTELSARDO

LA GUARDIOLA (€€)
One of the town's best restaurants in the top location in the Old Town, just below the Castello. The house delicacy is seafood, served on a terrace overlooking the sea.
✉ Piazza Bastione 4
☎ 079 470755;
www.ristorantelaguardiola.com
🕐 Jun–Sep daily; Oct–May Tue–Sun

SÁSSARI

BAR CAFFÈ FLORIAN (€)
Elegantly mirrored and muralled, both bar and the next-door restaurant are good spots for supping and dining. The bar/café has tables spilling out onto the pavement outside and Toulouse-Lautrec-style touches inside. The restaurant is more expensive but very good
✉ Via Roma 6 ☎ 079 200 8056 🕐 Mon–Sat

BAR RISTORANTE MOKADOR (€)
This buzzing little place is popular with the locals and a good choice for inexpensive snacks and drinks. On Fridays there is a happy hour from 7 to 9pm with *antipasti all'italiana* for an all-inclusive price of €5.
✉ Largo Cavallotti 2, off Piazza Castello, near Via Roma ☎ 079 235736

RISTORANTE LIBERTY (€€)
This elegantly restored restaurant, specialising in fish, was a little Liberty-style *palazzo*. Inside, choose between the Sala Afrodite or the Sala Apollo, each with appropriate murals. Alongside is their atmospheric wine/piano bar with a stream running down the stone steps into the tasting cellar.
✉ Piazza N Sauro 3 (off Corso Vittorio Emanuele) ☎ 079 236361 🕐 Tue–Sun

RISTORANTE PIZZERIA DA BRUNO (€)
This excellent restaurant is the saving grace of the otherwise unappealing Piazza Mazzotti. Good pizzas and pasta are served on an outdoor terrace with views towards the medieval town.
✉ Piazza Mazzotti 12 ☎ 079 235573

STINTINO

RISTORANTE DA ANTONIO (€€)
This welcoming family-run restaurant specialises in fish and seafood. The 'music bread' (▶ side panel) is excellent and the grilled fresh tuna is sublime. Portions tend to be generous and service is very attentive.
✉ Via Marco Polo 16 ☎ 079 523077 🕐 Summer only

SKIPPER (€)
Overlooking the port's armada of fishing boats, this is a friendly, popular bar. It serves good snack food, from salads and hamburgers to lasagne and fresh seafood – and home-made Sardinian pastries.
✉ Via Lungomare 57 ☎ 079 523460 🕐 Daily Jun–Sep

SARDINIAN BREAD

No meal is complete without some of the typical Sardinian bread. *Pane carasau* is the most famous, also known as 'music paper' (*carta da musica*). The wafer-thin, twice-baked delicacy was originally introduced by the Arabs in the 9th century, then adopted by the shepherds as it could keep for a long time in the pastures. It is especially delicious served with salt and warm olive oil and sprinkled with herbs.

69

The Northeast

Bars usually open around 7am for breakfast (*prima colazione*). A cappuccino and *cornetto* (croissant) is the usual Sard fare, which, incidentally, Sardinians almost never take sitting down. When in Sardinia, stand at the bar and join in. Lunch (*pranzo*) is traditionally the main meal of the day. By 1.30pm most people are tucking in and it can be a very leisurely affair. After all, everything stops for the siesta and businesses and shops close for up to four hours every afternoon. Dinner (*cena*) usually begins late, around 9pm (although earlier in rural areas). However, there are plenty of places that cater for visitors who like to dine earlier too.

BÁIA SARDINIA

TANIT (€€€)
This is the place to go if you want to push the boat out, literally. Overlooking this exclusive marina between Báia Sardinia and Porto Cervo, you are likely to be rubbing shoulders with the international jet set in this very elegant restaurant. A gourmet feast of fish and seafood specialities tops the menu, although Argentine beef also appears. The service is very attentive and the price is very high.
✉ Poltu Quatu ☎ 0789 95500 ☀ Summer daily from 7.30pm (bar from 6)

CANNIGIONE

L'ANCORA (€€)
This delightful restaurant is deservedly very popular. Antipasti include smoked tuna and lobster, the wood-burning oven makes delicious fresh pizzas to order and there's also an excellent selection of meat dishes. A good selection of wines is offered, as well as *mirto*, the traditional and potent myrtle berry liqueur of the island.
✉ Località La Conta, 1km north of Cannigione ☎ 0789 86086

COSTA SMERALDA

BAR BARETTO PIZZERIA (€)
The pizzas, salads and snacks here are excellent value, and are served outside on a pleasant terrace.
✉ Cala di Volpe, 07020 Porto Cervo ☎ 0789 86086

MAMA LATINA (€€)
This pizzeria/restaurant is one of the few to open all year round. Given the exclusive surroundings, dining here is a reasonable option with inexpensive pizzas in the front café and good salads and fish dishes on offer in the stylish dining room.
✉ Porto Cervo Marina ☎ 0789 91312 ☀ Apr–Sep daily; Oct–Mar Mon–Sat

ÍSOLA TAVOLARA

RISTORANTE DA TONINO (€€)
Dine regally at Tonino's – the present day 'King' of Tavolara. There is an enticing veranda on the beach and the speciality is fish and seafood, served with great aplomb.
✉ Via Tavolara 14 ☎ 0789 58570 ☀ Summer only

LA MADDALENA

LA GROTTA (€€)
This long-established family restaurant is rustic, atmospheric and always bustling. Fish and seafood are piled high in tantalising dishes such as *penne alla grotta* seafood pasta or *aragosta setteotto*, the signature lobster dish.
✉ Via Principe di Napoli 3 ☎ 0789 737228; www.lagrotta.it ☀ May–Sep

ÓLBIA

DA ANTONIO (€)
This stone-clad trattoria in the centre of Ólbia serves fixed-price menus in a pleasant laid-back environment. It is also a good pizzeria.

✉ Via Garibaldi 48 ☎ 0789 609082

LA LANTERNA DA GIACOMO (€–€€)

In the heart of Ólbia, this restaurant/pizzeria is in an intimate subterranean setting. Portions are extremely generous and the home-made puddings are especially delectable. Very good, attentive service.

✉ Via Olbia 13 ☎ 0789 23082 🕐 Summer daily; winter Thu–Tue

RISTORANTE GALLURA (€€)

This very popular restaurant's cuisine is a successful blend of the traditional and creative, using both fish and meat. Specialities include *anemoni di mare fritti* (fried sea urchins), rabbit in saffron, mussels – and delicious puddings. Extensive wine list.

✉ Corso Umberto 145 ☎ 0789 24648 🕐 Tue–Sun

RISTORANTE PIZZERIA L'ANCORA (€–€€)

On the seafront, this pleasant mid-range restaurant specialises in fresh fish, although there are also meat dishes on offer (including horse) and pizzas in the evening.

✉ Lungomare via Redipuglia ☎ 0789 205013; www.lancoraolbia.com

PALAU

LA TAVERNA (€€)

You'll find this atmospheric tavern in the town centre, very close to the port. Not surprisingly, the speciality is freshly caught fish and seafood. Set menus are available for fishy feasts.

✉ Via Rossini 6 ☎ 0789 709289 🕐 Jun–Sep dinner daily; Mar–May, Oct–Nov Wed–Sun

PORTO ROTONDO

ANTONELLA & GIGI (€€)

This rustic, family-run restaurant is very good value for the location. Expect classic dishes such as *insalata di mare* (seafood salad), *prosciutto e melone* (ham and melon), mixed grilled fish and a 'catch of the day'.

✉ Villaggio Juniperus ☎ 0789 34238 🕐 Wed–Mon 12–3, 7–11

SANTA TERESA DI GALLURA

CANNE AL VENTO (€€€)

Elegant seafood restaurant in the hotel of the same name. Come here for pasta with *bottarga*, grilled calamari, stuffed swordfish and other delicacies.

✉ Via Nazionale 23 ☎ 0789 754219 🕐 Apr–Oct

TÉMPIO PAUSÁNIA

IL GIARDINO (€€)

Centrally located, off Piazza Gallura, this traditional restaurant/pizzeria was established in 1926. Good grilled meat dishes are staples, along with some Sardinian specialities. The interior is a little functional but the open-air terrace is attractive.

✉ Via Cavour 1 ☎ 079 671247 🕐 Thu–Tue

PLACES TO EAT

Similar to mainland Italy, differences between the various types of restaurant are no longer so clearly defined. While a *ristorante* used to be an upmarket and expensive establishment and a *trattoria* was cheap and simple, the differences between the two have become increasingly blurred. Pizzerias, too, will often have other dishes such as pasta and salads on offer as well as pizzas alone. An *enoteca* is a wine bar which has a good selection of wines by the glass, accompanied by salamis, cheeses and a selection of snacks or light meals. You will also find the odd *birreria*, where you can get a beer (or glass of wine) with snacks and light meals. This is where local young people tend to hang out listening to loud music.

Cágliari and the South

PRICES

Prices are approximate for a double room, including breakfast and taxes:

€ = under €90
€€ = €90–€155
€€€ = €155–€250
€€€€ = over €250

Generally speaking, the cost of accommodation is lower than in mainland Italy – with the exception of the hotels in and around the Costa Smeralda, which are among the most expensive in the world. High-season tariffs usually apply between mid-July and mid-September. At other times the rates plummet and, if you have the flexibility, there are some excellent bargains on offer out of high season.

HOTEL A&R BUNDES JACK (€)

On the Via Roma with superb views out to the sea, this historic building with high ceilings, murano glass and antique tiles houses a characterful two-star hotel on the third floor (with lift). The family also runs the Bed & Breakfast Vittoria next door

✉ Via Roma 75 ☎ 070 657970 🕐 All year

HOTEL CALAMOSCA (€€–€€€)

This large beach hotel has an excellent position right on the seafront and is very convenient for Poetto. Most rooms have a balcony overlooking the garden or bay – there's a small supplement for the sea-facing rooms, but these are the ones to choose. There is a pleasant garden and direct access to two beaches.

✉ Viale Calamosca, 50 (about 2km from town) ☎ 070 371628; www.hotelcalamosca.it

LE MERIDIEN CHIA LAGUNA RESORT (€€€–€€€€)

Set in the beautiful bay of Chia, the resort offers elegant accommodation in rooms that have spectacular views to the sea, or, in family rooms in the Mediterranean garden, of Chia village.

✉ Località Chia, Domus de Maria ☎ 070 92391; www.le meridien-chialaguna.it 🕐 End Apr–Sep

T HOTEL (€€€)

This is Cágliari's first designer hotel. The 15-storey steel and glass round tower was designed by famous Milanese architect Marco Piva and opened in October 2005.

✉ Via dei Giudicati ☎ 070 47400; www.thotel.it

HOTEL RIVIERA (€€€)

This terracotta-coloured building is a landmark on the harbourfront and is the island's most chic hotel. The 44 rooms simply ooze style and comfort with luxurious marble bathrooms.

✉ Corso Battellieri 26 ☎ 078 854101; www.hotelriviera-carloforte.com 🕐 End Mar–Oct

HOTEL CRUCCURIS (€€–€€€)

This hotel is set among flower-filled gardens in the hills outside Villasimíus. The 45 rooms are arranged around the attractive freshwater swimming pool.

✉ Località Cruccuris (3km outside town) ☎ 070 798 9020; www.cruccurisresort.com

STELLA MARIS HOTEL (€€)

This hotel has a lovely setting overlooking Capo Carbonara. Pretty gardens lead down to the white sandy beach and there's also a freshwater pool. The rooms are traditionally furnished and the best have a sea view.

✉ Località Cruccuris (3km outside town) ☎ 070 798 9020; www.cruccurisresort.com

Oristano and the West

ABBASANTA

MANDRA EDERA FARM (€€)

Once purely an *agriturismo* restaurant, the farm is now a hotel with rooms with en suite facilities. Guests sit together at a large refectory-style table for meals. Good opportunities for horse-riding and excursions to nearby Nuraghe Losa.

✉ Via Dante 20 Abbasanta
☎ 0785 52710;
www.mandraedera.it
🕐 May–Dec

CÚGLIERI

HOTEL LA BAJA (€€–€€€)

This charming hotel is a mere stone's throw from the Sínis Peninsula at the foot of Monte Ferru. Nearly all of the 29 rooms have a balcony and sea view, as does the swimming pool. Sunny colours predominate and the good restaurant has an attractive veranda overlooking the sea.

✉ Via Scirocco 20, Santa Caterina di Pittinuri ☎ 0785 389149; www.hotellabaja.it

MARINA DI TORRE GRANDE

SPINNAKER (€–€€)

Set among pine trees on the seashore, this well-equipped campsite also has comfortable bungalows, some of which have kitchens. There's also a private beach.

✉ Torre Grande Pontile
☎ 0783 22074;
www.campingspinnaker.com
🕐 All year

ORISTANO

DUOMO ALBERGO (€–€€)

This historic 17th-century building in the old centre has 10 spacious, bright rooms, the best of which are set around the charming courtyard. There is a good restaurant and pleasant bar.

✉ Via Vittorio Emanuele 34
☎ 0783 778061;
www.hotelduomo.net

MISTRAL 2 (€–€€)

This modern hotel is right in the centre of town. There are 132 functional yet comfortable rooms, a swimming pool and a pleasant restaurant.

✉ Via XX Settembre, 34
☎ 0783 210389

RIOLA SARDO

AGRITURISMO SU LAU (€)

A peaceful, rural retreat with six very comfortable rooms set amid fruit orchards. Dinner in the farmhouse, prepared with fresh seasonal produce, is available on request.

✉ Via Luigino Bellu 24
☎ 0783 410897

HOTEL LUCREZIA (€€)

This small historic hotel, in the heart of the village, has the traditional wine cellar, well and bread oven in its garden, surrounded by centuries-old trees. The seven rooms are traditionally furnished, but also have modern facilities, including internet connection.

✉ Via Roma 14a ☎ 0783 412078; www.hotellucrezia.it

HOTEL SEASONS

Many hotels, especially in coastal areas, are open only during the summer season, usually May/June to September. In some there is a minimum stay requirement and sometimes half or full board is mandatory.

73

Núoro and the East

BED AND BREAKFAST

B&Bs are becoming increasingly popular in Sardinia. Most are generally very comfortable and clean; some offer shared use of bathrooms, while others have en suite facilities. For more information visit Bed & Breakfast Sardegna at www.bebsardegna.it

CALA GONONE

HOTEL COSTA DORADA (€€€)

This family-run small hotel is a little jewel set among flower-filled gardens. There are 23 comfortable rooms in traditional Sardinian style and a vine-shaded dining terrace with splendid views over the Gulf of Orosei.

✉ Lungomare Palamsera 45 ☎ 0784 93332; www.hotelcostadorada.it ⏱ Apr–Oct

HOTEL POP (€–€€)

Opposite the port, this friendly, welcoming three-star hotel is run by the charismatic Anglophile Simone Spanu and his family. Service is excellent, rooms are modern and clean and every kind of excursion can be arranged.

✉ Via Marco Polo 2 ☎ 0784 93185

DORGALI

HOTEL IL QUERCETO (€€)

Decorated in typical mountain style, this three-star hotel has airy, spacious rooms overlooking woodland. The gardens are attractive and there are tennis courts.

✉ Via Lamarmora 4 ☎ 0784 96509; www.ilquerceto.com ⏱ Apr–Oct

MONTE ORTOBENE

CASA SOLOTTI (€)

This B&B is a friendly, family establishment with five rooms – three of which have balconies with glorious views. All rooms are quiet and comfortable, and surrounded by pleasant gardens.

✉ Monte Ortobene ☎ 0784 33954; www.casasolotti.it

FRATELLI SACCHI (€–€€)

Near to the top of Monte Ortobene, this is a good base for immersing yourself in great views in the countryside. There are 22 comfortable, rustic rooms, some with balconies.

✉ Monte Ortobene ☎ 0784 31200 ⏱ Apr–Oct

OLIENA

HOTEL SU GOLOGONE (€€€)

Like a balcony over the Valle di Lanaittu, this is one of Sardinia's most lovely hotels/restaurants. There are 68 rooms, decorated in harmony with the arts and crafts of the region, and most have a balcony.

✉ Località Su Gologone (7km northeast of Oliena) ☎ 0784 287512; www.sugologone.it ⏱ Mid-Mar to 5 Nov

SANTU LUSSÚRGIU

ANTICA DIMORA DEL GRUCCIONE (€–€€)

This lovely 17th-century mansion is Spanish in design and filled with antiques. It is an *albergo diffuso*, consisting of a main house and several other buildings in the neighbourhood.

✉ Via Michele Obinu 31 ☎ 0783 552035; www.anticadimora.com

Sássari and the Northwest

ALGHERO

AGRITURISMO VESSUS (€)

This family-run hotel has a beautiful setting in olive groves and gardens, and the traditional-style rooms encircle the swimming pool. The very good restaurant specialises in Sardinian food.

✉ SS 292 Km1.85 per Villanova Monteleone (3km south of Alghero) ☎ 079 973 5018; www.vessus.it

HOTEL SAN FRANCESCO (€€)

A former convent, this is Alghero's only hotel in the old town and a perfect retreat. There are 21 clean and quiet rooms, the best of which overlook the old cloisters of the Chiesa di San Francesco.

✉ Via Ambrogio Machin 2 ☎ 079 980330; www.sanfrancescohotel.com

HOTEL VILLA LAS TRONAS (€€€€)

Spectacularly located on a private promontory overlooking the sea, this former Italian royal family holiday home is Alghero's most luxurious hotel. Antiques, marbled halls, chandeliers and rich brocades ooze opulence in this 19th-century palace.

✉ Lungomare Valencia 1 ☎ 079 981818; www.hotelvillalastronas.it

BOSA

CORTE FIORITA (€–€€)

Made up of three different historical buildings, this collection of *alberghi* is in the heart of Bosa. The rooms are rustic, light and spacious with tiled floors, exposed stone walls and tasteful fabrics. There's a small supplement for a balcony and river views.

✉ Lungo Temo De Gasperi 45 ☎ 0785 377058; www.albergo-diffuso.it

HOTEL SA PISCHEDDA (€–€€)

Set in a *palazzo* across the Ponte Vecchio bridge, this charming hotel has some rooms with frescoed ceilings. Some have terraces and balconies overlooking the river and all are air-conditioned.

✉ Via Roma 8 ☎ 0785 373065; www.hotelsapischedda.it ⏰ Dec–Oct

CASTELSARDO

HOTEL RIVIERA DA FOFÒ (€€)

Set on the road across from the town beach, the views from here of the old town are lovely. Rooms are comfortable and modern and some have balconies.

✉ Via Lungomare Anglona 1 ☎ 079 470143; www.hotelriviera.net

SÁSSARI

HOTEL VITTORIO EMANUELE (€–€€)

In the heart of the city, this pleasing *palazzo* has been fully restored, and now has carefully furnished, comfortable rooms where style veers to modern minimalist, but with murals.

✉ Corso Vittorio Emanuele II, 100/102 ☎ 079 235538; www.hotelvittorioemanuele.ss.it

AGRITURISMO

Agriturismi are cottages or farmhouses usually located in the countryside. They are normally more expensive than B&Bs, but the best have locally grown, organic produce and offer excursions and horse riding. For more information contact Agriturismo di Sardegna ☎ 0783 411660; www.agriturismosardegna.it

The Northeast

CANNIGIONE

HOTEL BAJA (€€€)
The interior here is a vision in white and minimalist in style. There are 61 spacious rooms and one penthouse suite.
✉ Via Nazionale ☎ 0789 892041; www.hotelbaja.it
🕐 Apr–Sep

LI CAPANNI (€€€)
Lying between Cannigione and Palau, this oasis of calm, owned by musician Peter Gabriel, has 5ha of grounds and its own secluded beach. The charming accommodation is in six terracotta-coloured cottages.
✉ Golfo di Saline ☎ 0789 86041; www.licapanni.com
🕐 May–Sep

COSTA SMERALDA

CERVO HOTEL (€€€€)
The most 'villagey' of all the Starwood hotels, this one is right in the heart of Porto Cervo on the Piazzetta, with views over the marina. Rooms are rustic, in an elegant, understated way, and most have their own terrace or balcony with lovely views.
✉ Piazzetta Porto Cervo ☎ 0789 931111; www.sheraton.com 🕐 Apr–Oct

HOTEL PITRIZZA (€€€€)
Small and exclusive, this villa-style hotel is the perfect hideaway for couples. It manages to be understated yet very sophisticated, and has its own private beach.
✉ Porto Cervo ☎ 0789 930111; www.luxurycollection. com/hotelpitrizza 🕐 May–Oct

ÓLBIA

HOTEL CAVOUR (€–€€)
This small, tastefully refurbished hotel in the centre of Ólbia's old town is mostly cool white with pastel shades. There's on-site parking.
✉ Via Cavour 22 ☎ 0789 204033; www.cavourhotel.it

HOTEL CENTRALE (€€)
This very central hotel was totally refurbished at the end of 2006. Clean and welcoming with plenty of marble and minimalist clean lines, the rooms are pleasant and comfortable.
✉ Corso Umberto 85 ☎ 0789 23017; www.hotelcentraleolbia.it

PORTO ROTONDO

HOTEL ABI D'ORU (€€€–€€€€)
This salmon-coloured resort stands on a beautiful bay. The rooms are comfortable, uncluttered and of a good size, and most have sea views. In the grounds there is a large freshwater swimming pool and a lake.
✉ Golfo di Marinella (6km from Porto Rotondo) ☎ 0789 309019; www.altamarea.it
🕐 Apr–Oct

SANTA TERESA DI GALLURA

MARINARO (€€)
In a quiet street that is in the centre yet close to the beach, this pleasant peach-coloured hotel has smart and airy bedrooms.
✉ Via Angioy 48 ☎ 0789 754112; www.hotelmarinaro.it

Shopping

CÁGLIARI AND THE SOUTH

The best all-round shopping of the region is in the capital, Cágliari. Note that shops are usually open from 9 to 1, close for a lengthy lunch/siesta and reopen from 4 or 5 till 7 or 8.

For clothes and boutiques, from Bastione San Remy take the Via Manno down to Piazza Yenne. Via Roma also has some designer shops and the department store Rinascente.

The main street, Largo Carlo Felice, has some shops and plenty of African traders selling handbags, sunglasses and all kinds of other accessories – some of which are a bit suspect.

JENNA E LUA

This little shop is crammed full of Sardinian delicacies such as cheese, salamis, wines and *dolci sardi*. It is also a good place to pick up items of ceramics and other prettily packaged souvenirs.
✉ Corso Vittorio Emanuele 27
☎ 070 682161

ISOLA

The Institute for Sardinian Handicrafts' headquarters is in Cágliari (▶ side panel).
✉ Via Bacaredda 184
☎ 070 404791;
www.regione.sardegna.it/isola
🅖 Mon–Sat morning

RINASCENTE

A quality branch of the Italian department store chain.
✉ Via Roma 143 ☎ 070
60451 🅖 Mon–Fri 9–8.30, Sat 9–9, Sun 10–9

MARKETS

For antiques and bric-à-brac, there are morning markets at Piazza del Carmine on the first Sunday of the month, at Piazza Carlo Alberto on the second and fourth Sundays and a fleamarket at Bastione San Remy every Sunday except during August. For food and household goods, visit the San Benedetto covered market (Via Francesco Cocco Ortu, north of the Castello; open mornings Mon–Fri and all day Sat).

ORISTANO AND THE WEST

ORISTANO

CANTINA SOCIALE DELLA VERNACCIA

The area is renowned for its white Vernaccia wine and local winegrowers bring their grapes here to be crushed. You can buy from the source in the cantina shop.
✉ Via Oristano 149, Rimedi
☎ 0783 33155 🅖 Summer Mon–Fri 8–1, 4–6.30; winter 8–1, 3.30–6

ISOLA

Oristano's outlet, showcasing traditional handicrafts (▶ side panel).
✉ Piazza Eleonora 18
☎ 0783 779025

MARKETS

In Oristano there are morning markets in Via Mazzini and Via Costa (Mon–Sat) and on the first

TRADITIONAL CRAFTS

Each region of Sardinia has its own crafts and there has been a recent revival in traditions such as carpet weaving, ceramics, embroidery, jewellery and other cottage industries. Some of the touristy shops vary in quality so it's always a good idea to compare prices and quality. The **Istituto Sardo Organizzazione Lavoro Artigiano** – (ISOLA for short) – has outlets in places such as Cágliari, Núoro, Porto Cervo, Oristano, Alghero and Sássari. Here you will find a good range of handicrafts and each piece is authenticated.

WINES AND SPIRITS

Wine production has a long history – probably dating back to before the time of the Phoenicians. Vermentino grapes make excellent white wines, while the Sardinia's best-known, full-bodied red wines are made from the Cannonau grape. Good fortified wines include Vernaccia (mostly from Oristano area) and Malvasia dessert wine (around Bosa). The national liqueur is *mirto*, made from the fruit of the myrtle bush, and there is also a version of the Amalfi coast's *limoncello* known in Sardinia as *limoncino* – sweet and just as pungent and best served over ice. The island version of grappa is extremely potent, made also from grape skins, but is known as *fil'e ferru*.

EMBROIDERY

Intricate lacework, wall hangings and carpets are highly prized. Especially fine are the wool carpets woven around Núoro province, where Ággius and Témpio Pausánia in particular excel with their geometric designs.

Saturday of the month an antiques/bric-à-brac market in Piazza Eleonora.

SENEGHE

ENOGASTRONOMIA DEL MONTIFERRU
Seneghe is the heartland of Sardinia's finest olive oil. The Sartos brand is a winner of the 'Ercole', Italy's most prestigious award. Pick up some bottles and other specialities of the area here.
✉ Corso Umberto 141/b; at the junction of Riola Sardo bear right, signposted Seneghe ☎ 0783 54450 🕓 Mon–Fri 8.30–1, 3.30–7

NÚORO AND THE EAST

DORGALI

ESCA DOLCIARIA
An excellent family-run pastry shop that specialises in gourmet sweets, ranging from typical pastries of the Dorgali region to more traditional Sardinian confections.
✉ Viale Kenney ☎ 0784 94472 🕓 Mon–Sat

NÚORO

ISOLA
The Núoro outlet of the reputable handmade crafts association (▶ panel, page 77).
✉ Corso Garibaldi 58 ☎ 078 433581 🕓 Mon–Sat 9–1, 4–8

TAVOLA DEGLI ANTICHI
The place to come for gourmet delicacies in

Núoro. Barbágian specialities on sale include *aranzada di Núoro* (candied orange peel and honey) and almond biscuits known as *s/aranzata*.
✉ Via Trieste 70 ☎ 078 435501

SÁSSARI AND THE NORTHWEST

ALGHERO

There is a wide range of boutiques for clothes, shoes and leather goods, plus shops selling locally crafted ceramics, pottery, cork and hand-woven baskets. There is also a huge choice of jewellery shops, mostly specialising in the local red coral. The modern side of town starts at the Via XX Settembre, where there are larger shops, perfumeries and boutiques. During the summer many shops stay open until midnight.

MARKETS
There's a daily fresh fish, fruit and vegetable market in Via Sássari; a large street market on Wednesday morning and a collectors' market on the last Sunday in the month. Also, on the last Saturday of the month, don't miss the arts, crafts and antiques market on the Piazza Cívico. In July and August, late night market stalls line the seafront on Lungomare Dante.

SELLA & MOSCA VINEYARD
This vineyard produces some of the island's top quality wines. There are

free daily guided tours plus the chance to buy red, white and rosé from the well-stocked shop.
✉ **Outside town on road close to the airport** ☎ 079 997700
🕐 Jun–Sep

SÁSSARI

Most of Sássari's shops are located on the Corso Vittorio Emanuele and on Via Roma. There is an antiques fair in Piazza Santa Caterina on the last Sunday of each month (Sep–Jun 8–1). From April to May there is a huge art and antiques fair, attended by some of the island's top antique dealers.

BAGELLA

One of Sássari's oldest shops specialises in authentic, well-made traditional Sardinian clothing, such as velvet suits, shirts, leather accessories and boots.
✉ **Corso Vittorio Emanuele 20**
☎ 079 235033; www.bagella.it
🕐 Mon–Sat 9–1, 5–8

GOLDEN POINT

This lingerie shop full of sexy undies and beachware is in the 15th-century Casa di Rienzo with stunning ceilings, mullion windows and frescoes. It offers good value for money while retaining a much more expensive-looking style.
✉ **Corso Vittorio Emanuele 41**

MURA (DI ELISABETTA E LUISA BRANCA)

A chic gift shop specialising in jewellery, silver, decorative objects and some antiques, at a

broad spectrum of prices.
✉ **Via Roma 12** ☎ 079 2353 32

MARKETS

Sássari has several markets, among them a covered market for fish (closed Mon), which also has vegetables and meat. There's a Sardinian handicrafts market in front of the Garibaldi statue, also closed on Mondays. The daily morning market (closed Sun) in Piazza Tola sells mostly clothes and household goods. The main food market is a little farther out from the centre on Via Mercato (mornings only).

THE NORTHEAST

The pretty resorts of Palau, Santa Teresa di Gallura, Báia Sardinia and Cannigione might lack the glamour and exclusivity of Porto Cervo and Porto Rotondo – where you'll find the usual range of top designer brands – but many visitors prefer their more laid-back feel. Each has its own supply of souvenir shops and night markets (the best is in Palau and stays open until 1am in peak season).

LA MADDALENA

SARDEGNA DA MANGIARE E DA BERE

This is an Aladdin's cave of Sardinian specialities. There is everything here, from cheese and salamis to pasta, *dolci sardi*, wines and *mirto* liqueur, all temptingly displayed.
✉ **Piazza Garibaldi 10**
☎ 0789 73108

JEWELLERY

The island is famous for its intricate filigree gold and silver craftsmanship and there are some beautiful pieces on offer. Alghero is famous for the deep red coral that's found off the nearby Riviera del Corallo coast. Fishing for the coral is both strictly regulated and dangerous and, as you would expect, jewellery crafted from this is expensive, especially when combined with filigree.

IN THE RESORTS

Some of the resorts have night markets, including Cannigione. The best is in Palau and it stays open until 1am in peak season.

Cágliari

BAR ETIQUETTE

It's always cheaper to stand at the bar than sit at a table. You pay at the separate cash desk (*cassa*) for your order and then take your receipt to the bar and repeat your order. Choosing to sit at a table means that the waiter will quickly take your order. What you shouldn't do is pay at the bar and then sit down with your drink. However, once you have elected to have waiter service you can sit for as long as you like – within reason.

BARS AND CAFÉS

Café society is alive and well in this city and there are several under the arcades of the Via Roma. Piazza Yenne is also a lively meeting place and, in summer, the beach at Poetto is the place to be for open-air bars. Castello, too, has new bars opening all the time and is magical also for its views across the 'Bay of Angels'.

CAFFÈ DEGLI SPIRITI

This café on the terrace at Bastione San Remy is a great place for a drink or snack while admiring the lovely views. DJs and live music in summer.
✉ Bastione San Remy

CAFFÈ LIBRARIUM NOSTRUM

Great location by the castle ramparts; live music in summer.
✉ Via Santa Croce 33 ☎ 070 650943 ◎ Tue–Sun

DE CANDIA BAR/ RESTAURANT

Good snacks are available, and on summer nights there's live music from 11.
✉ Via Marco de Candia 1–3, just by Bastione San Remy

IL MERLO PARLANTE

Just off the Corso Vittorio Emanuele, this buzzing *birreria* (pub) is very popular with students.
✉ Via Portoscalas 69 ☎ 070 653981 ◎ Tue–Sun

PERFORMANCE VENUES

For details of performances, pick up a free listings paper from the tourist office. The Box Office agency (Viale Regina Margherita 43 ☎ 070 657428; www.boxofficesardegna.it) sells tickets for events at Cágliari's major venues.

ANFITEATRO ROMANO

Open-air music, dance and concerts in summer with international performers. Tickets available in person from the Anfiteatro, Via Frà Ignazio da Laconi, or from Teatro Lirico or Box Office agency.
✉ Viale Sant'Ignazio da Laconi

EXMA COMPLEX

Concerts and recitals are staged here throughout the year. In summer there are open-air concerts for both classical and jazz.
✉ Via San Lucifero 71 ☎ 070 666399

FIERA CAMPIONARIA

This venue in the east of the city hosts open-air rock concerts in summer.
✉ Viale Diaz 221

TEATRO ALFIERI

This theatre stages classical drama (including Shakespeare), especially during the winter. Most productions are in Italian.
✉ Via della Pineta 29 ☎ 070 301378

TEATRO LIRICO

For opera, ballet and classical music, this is Cágliari's most important venue. The classical music, opera and ballet repertoire season is from November to July.
✉ Via Sant'Alenixedda ☎ 070 408 2130; www.teatroliricodicagliari.it

Around the Island

BARS AND CLUBS

ALGHERO

In high summer there are plenty of clubs and discos, particularly along the Lungomare.

POCO LOCO
Come here for live music and bowling.
✉ Via Gramsci 8, just off seafront ☎ 079 973 1034

COSTA SMERALDA

BILLIONAIRE CLUB
Flavio Briatore's Moroccan fantasy is the best-known of the trio of exclusive clubs around Porto Cervo where the glitterati congregate. Note that no cameras are allowed.
✉ Località Alto Pevero; www.billionaireclub.it ☎ 0789 94192 ◐ Jul–Sep

SOPRAVENTO
This club has occasional live bands and is also one of the biggest discos on the whole coast.
✉ Località Golfo di Pevero ☎ 0789 94717 ◐ Jun to mid-Sep 10.30pm–6am

SOTTOVENTO
No less exclusive than the Sopravento, if smaller, with a piano bar.
✉ Località Golfo di Pevero ☎ 0789 92443 ◐ Jun to mid-Sep 10.30pm–6am

NÚORO

BOCA CHICA
Núoro's only club has a Mexican theme and plays Latin music.
✉ Via Mughina 94 ☎ 329 3120010

SÁSSARI

Sássari has a thriving cultural scene with three theatres, and, as you would expect from a university town, plenty of buzzing bars, especially along the Via Roma and in Piazza Castello.

PIANO BAR LIBERTY
In a small piazza adjacent to the Corso Vittorio Emanuele, this popular wine/piano bar has a stream running down the stone steps into the tasting cellar.
✉ Piazza N Sauro 3 ☎ 079 236361 ◐ Tue–Sun lunch and evening

VILLASIMÍUS

CAFÉ DEL PORTO
The only café/bar at the marina, and buzzing from 10.30pm in season.
✉ Porto di Villasimíus ☎ 070 797 8036 ◐ Daily 7am–2am

PERFORMANCE VENUES

ALGHERO

TEATRO CIVICO
Stages opera, concerts and plays throughout the year.
✉ Piazza Vittorio Emanuele ☎ 079 997 800

COSTA SMERALDA

CHIESA DI STELLA MARIS
This whitewashed church is modern but contains El Greco's *Mater Dolorosa*, and is the atmospheric setting for classical music concerts in the summer.
✉ La Piazzetta, Porto Cervo

Sports and Activities

BOATING AND WATER SPORTS

Sailing is the royal pastime – especially on the Costa Smeralda – where it is possible to rent a yacht, even if you haven't brought it with you. Along the Golfo di Orosei, if you want to explore the coast alone, you can hire a motorboat in Cala Gonone from one of the companies that has kiosks on the harbour front.

THE *ANDREA JENSEN*

Not only can you enjoy an excursion aboard this traditional sailing boat, but you can also help out with steering and sail-rigging; no prior experience necessary.
✉ Alghero ☎ 33390 708139; www.ajsailing.com

AZIENDA MARE E NATURA

Boat excursions from Stintino to Parco Nazionale dell'Asinara, including a Land Rover drive.
✉ Via Sássari 77, Stintino ☎ 079 520097

BOSA DIVING CENTRE

PADI diving courses are available as well as boat excursions.
✉ Piazza Paul Harris, Bosa Marina ☎ 07895 375649

MARINASARDA

Boat hire, from a 4.5m Capelli to a 12.5m Cranchi speedboat. The smaller boats are self-skippered, the larger include a skipper.
✉ The 'Old Port', in the southern part of Porto Cervo village near Hotel Cervo ☎ 0789 67498

LA SCHIUMARA BEACH

Watersports firm run by Paul and Andreana (English-speaking). Sailing and windsurfing courses, also waterskiing and banana boat rides.
✉ La Schiumara Beach, Cannigione ☎ 338 390 5706

GOLF

For golf enthusiasts, Sardinia has two of Europe's most beautiful 18-hole courses, Pevero Golf Club and Is Molas on the Costa Smeralda.

CLUB IS ARENAS

An 18-hole course on the west coast, north of Oristano.
✉ Is Arenas Golf & Country Club, Località Pineta Is Arenas, Narbolia ☎ 0783 522036

GOLF CLUB VILLASIMÍUS

Modern nine-hole course in the southeast.
✉ Via degli Oleandri, Villasimíus ☎ 0362 354481

IS MOLAS GOLF HOTEL

Located 30km from Cágliari on the southwest coast near Santa Margherita di Pula, the microclimate of this region makes this beautiful course accessible all year round.
✉ S195, Località Is Molas, Santa Margherita di Pula ☎ 070 924 1006

PEVERO GOLF CLUB

Designed by Robert Trent Jones in 1972, the course has a spectacular setting overlooking the sea.

✉ Località Cala di Volpe between Pevero Gulf and Cala di Volpe bay ☎ 0789 958000

HIKING AND SKIING

There is wonderful mountain terrain to be explored and hiked over, especially in the Gennargentu and Supramonte mountain ranges. There is bolted climbing too, which is very popular around Cala Gonone. Tourist offices have detailed maps for hiking in these areas and will advise on the degree of difficulty – many are strenuous and you need to be well-equipped. There is skiing in the winter at Fonni, but the slopes are better suited to cross-country than downhill skiing.

WALKING ORGANISATIONS

There are several guided walks organisations, notably the following:
Cooperativa Ghivine covers the area around the Golfo di Orosei.
✉ Via Lamarmora 69/e, Dorgali ☎ 0784 96721
Cooperativa Gorropu arranges excursions to the Gola Su Gorrruppu as well as caving and canyoning.
✉ Via Sa Preda Lada 2, Urzulei ☎ 0782 649282
Servizi Turistici Corrasi has guided walking tours and treks in the Gennargentu and Supramonte.
✉ Piazza Santa Maria 30, Oliena ☎ 0784 287144
Italian Alpine Club
☎ 070 667877;
www.caica.sardegna.it

HORSE RIDING

For those who would rather let the horse take the strain, pony trekking is very popular in the Barbágia region and plenty of seaside resorts offer the opportunity to canter along the sands on the sparkling seashore. Many hotels offer riding excursions, such as Mandra Edera Farm and Ala Birdi in Oristano. For more information, visit www.sardegnacavalli.it
☎ 079 787852.

SWIMMING, SURFING AND DIVING

Swimming is good virtually throughout the island and wind- or kite-surfing is popular everywhere, although the winds are especially good on the north coast. The west coast has some terrific surf at the beaches around Buggerru. Snorkellers and divers will find an underwater paradise in the limpid waters and there are many schools and PADI-registered diving outfits, especially around the Golfo di Orosei. Cala Gonone is a good centre for diving and there are several clubs.

ARGONAUTA

On offer are snorkelling tours accompanied by professional guides; dives on World War II wrecks and caverns; shallow dives; night dives; and PADI courses at all levels.
✉ Via dei Lecci 10, Cala Gonone
☎ 0784 93046;
www.argonauta.it

WILD HORSES

The Sards are among Italy's finest riders, especially in the 'Wild West' – Oristano province. The best place to see the daredevil riders in action is at one of the region's festivals, particularly Sa Sartiglia, held in Oristano at Carnival time, and S'Ardia, held in Sedilo in July. The origins of the Sartiglia go back to knightly tournaments, and today's riders have to demonstrate their skill with a lance, trying to spear hanging objects at speed. The S'Ardia is like a more extreme version of Siena's Palio races, with 100 of the bravest horsemen rampaging full tilt around the village to the accompaniment of roaring crowds and riflemen shooting into the air hundreds of cartridges filled with black dust.

83

SARDINIA
practical matters

WHAT YOU NEED

	UK	Germany	USA	Netherlands	Spain
● Required — Some countries require a passport to remain valid for a minimum					
○ Suggested — period (usually at least six months) beyond the date of entry –					
▲ Not required — contact their consulate, embassy or travel agent for details.					
Passport/national identity card	●	●	●	●	●
Visa (regulations can change – check before you travel)	▲	▲	▲	▲	▲
Onward or return ticket	○	○	●	○	○
Health inoculations (tetanus and polio)	▲	▲	▲	▲	▲
Health documentation (reciprocal agreement: ➤ 90, Health)	●	●	▲	●	●
Travel insurance	○	○	○	○	○
Driving licence (national or international)	●	●	●	●	●
Car insurance certificate (if own car)	●	●	●	●	●
Car registration document (if own car)	●	●	●	●	●

WHEN TO GO

Average figures for Sardinia

High season

Low season

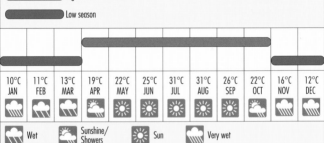

10°C JAN	11°C FEB	13°C MAR	19°C APR	22°C MAY	25°C JUN	31°C JUL	31°C AUG	26°C SEP	22°C OCT	16°C NOV	12°C DEC

Wet — Sunshine/Showers — Sun — Very wet

TIME DIFFERENCES

GMT	Sardinia	Germany	USA (NY)	Netherlands	Spain
12 noon	1pm	1pm	7am	1pm	1pm

TOURIST OFFICES

In the UK
ENIT
1 Princes Street
London W1B 2AY
☎ 020 7408 1254

In the USA
ENIT
630 Fifth Avenue
Suite 1565, New York
NY 10111
☎ 212/245-561

In Italy
Italian State Tourist Board
Via Marghera 2/6
00185 Rome
☎ 06 49711
www.enit.it
www.sardegnaturismo.it

ARRIVING

Cágliari Airport
Kilometres to city centre

6 kilometres

Journey times	
🚆	N/A
🚌	10 minutes
🚕	8 minutes

Ólbia Airport
Kilometres to city centre

5 kilometres

Journey times	
🚆	N/A
🚌	10 minutes
🚕	7 minutes

Alghero Airport
Kilometres to city centre

10 kilometres

Journey times	
🚆	N/A
🚌	20 minutes
🚕	15 minutes

TIME

Sardinia is on GMT +1, making it 1 hour ahead of the UK, 6 hours ahead of New York and 9 hours ahead of Los Angeles. Italy puts its clocks forward one hour between April and October.

CUSTOMS

YES

From another EU country for personal use (guidelines)
800 cigarettes
200 cigars
1kg of tobacco
10 litres of spirits (over 22%)
20 litres of aperitifs
90 litres of wine, of which 60 litres can be sparkling wine
110 litres of beer

From a non-EU country for your personal use, the allowances are:
200 cigarettes OR
50 cigars OR
250g of tobacco
1 litre of spirits (over 22%)
2 litres of intermediary products (eg sherry) and sparkling wine
2 litres of still wine
60ml of perfume
250ml of eau de toilette
Other goods up to a total value of €175

Travellers under the age of 17 are not entitled to the tobacco and alcohol allowances.

NO

Drugs, firearms, ammunition, offensive weapons, obscene material, unlicensed animals. Wildlife souvenirs may be illegal; check your home country's regulations.

MONEY

The legal currency of Sardinia is the euro (€), which is split into 100 cents. Euro notes are issued in denominations of 5, 10, 20, 50, 100, 200 and 500, and coins in 1, 2, 5, 10, 20 and 50 cents and 1 and 2 euros. All euro coins and notes are accepted in all member states. Most major traveller's cheques can be exchanged at kiosks (*cambio*) at the airports and large hotels. Credit cards are widely accepted and cash withdrawals can be made from ATMs with a transaction fee. Note that credit cards are rarely accepted in B&Bs and *agriturismi*, and in many small establishments cash is preferred.

CONSULATES/EMBASSIES

UK
☎ 070 828628
www.fco.gov.uk

USA
☎ 06 46741
www.usembassy.it

Germany
☎ 070 307229
www.konsulate.de

Spain
☎ 06 684 04 01

TOURIST OFFICES

Alghero
✉ Piazza Porta Terra 9, at the top end of the Giardini Pubblici ☎ 079 979054 ⏰ Apr–Oct Mon–Sat 8–8, Sun 9–1; Nov–Mar Mon–Sat 8–2

Cágliari
Information Point
Near the waterfront just to the west of Via Roma, with helpful English-speaking staff.
✉ Piazza Matteotti 9 ☎ 070 669255; www.comune.cagliari.it ⏰ Mon–Fri 8.30–1.30, 2–8, Sat–Sun 8–8 (times vary)

There is another tourist office at the eastern end of Via Roma:
✉ Piazza Deffenu 9 ☎ 070 604241 ⏰ Mon–Sat 9–1.30

Núoro
✉ Piazza Italia 19 ☎ 0784 30083; www.enteturismo.nuoro.it ⏰ Mon–Sat 9–1, 4–7

There is also a useful independent Punta Informa:
✉ Corso Garibaldi 155 ☎ 0784 38777 ⏰ Mon–Fri 9–1, 3.30–7 (sometimes also Sat monring)

Ólbia
Azienda Autonoma Soggiorno e Turismo
✉ Via Nanni ☎ 0789 21453; www.olbia.it ⏰ Mid-Jun to mid-Sep Mon–Sat 8.30–1, 4.30–7.30, Sun 8.30–1; mid-Sep to mid-Jun Mon–Sat 8.30–1

Oristano
✉ Piazza Eleonora d'Arborea 19 ☎ 0783 36831 ⏰ Summer Mon–Sat 9–1, 4–7; winter Mon–Fri 9–1, 4–7, Sat 9–1

Sássari
✉ Via Roma 62 (opposite end of road from Piazza Italia) ☎ 079 231777; www.comune.sassari.it ⏰ Mon–Thu 9–1.30, 4–6, Fri 9–1.30

ELECTRICITY

The power supply is 220 volts AC. Plugs are two-round-pin Continental types. UK, North American and Australasian visitors will need an adaptor. North American visitors will also need a voltage transformer for appliances operating on 100–120 volts.

NATIONAL HOLIDAYS

J	F	M	A	M	J	J	A	S	O	N	D
2		(2)	1 (3)	1	1		1			1	3

1 Jan	New Year's Day
6 Jan	Epiphany
Mar/Apr	Good Friday and Easter Monday
25 Apr	Liberation Day
1 May	Labour Day
2 Jun	Republic Day
15 Aug	Ferragosto (Assumption)
1 Nov	Ognissanti (All Saints)
8 Dec	Immaculate Conception
25 Dec	Christmas Day
26 Dec	St Stephen's Day

OPENING HOURS

○ Shops
● Offices
● Banks
● Pharmacies
● Museums/Monuments
● Post Offices

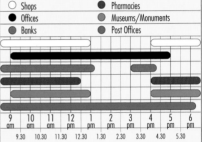

9 am	10 am	11 am	12	1 pm	2 pm	3 pm	4 pm	5 pm	6 pm
9.30	10.30	11.30	12.30	1.30	2.30	3.30	4.30	5.30	

Shops are usually open Mon–Sat 8–1, 4 or 5–7 or 8. Some close Monday morning and all shops, except the odd food shop, are closed on Sundays. Big department stores in Cágliari and Sássari have continuous opening 9–8.30.
Some museums are closed on Mondays, although many of these will open daily in high season. Archaeological sites are usually open from 9 to 1 hour before sunset. Many smaller museums and places of interest have very reduced hours during winter and some close down completely.
In bigger towns there is usually a pharmacy that is open all night – addresses are given on pharmacy doors or listed in the local paper.
Post offices are open all day Mon–Fri but only in the morning on Saturdays, until about 1pm.
Churches usually open 7am or 8am–noon and 4pm–7pm. Smaller ones only open for morning and evening services.

TIPS/GRATUITIES

Yes ✓	No ✗	
Restaurants (service included)	✓	Change
Restaurants (service not included)	✓	10%
Cafés/bars (service not included)	✓	Change/10%
Taxis	✓	Discretionary
Tour guides	✓	Discretionary
Porters	✓	€1–€2
Chambermaids	✓	Discretionary
Hairdressers	✓	10%
Toilets	✓	Discretionary

PUBLIC TRANSPORT

 Island buses Sardinia has an extensive network of buses, which links not only villages and towns but also beaches (although these routes, like those to archaeological sites, operate only during the summer). The main operator ARST (Azienda Regionale Sarda Trasporti; www.arst.sardegna.it) has a good service covering routes from the main cities – Cágliari, Sássari, Oristano, Ólbia and Núoro. A trip from Cágliari to Sássari takes about 3.5 hours and costs about €15. For bus routes and timetables, see www.orariautobus.it.

 Trains Trains in Sardinia are rather slow and the rail network is limited. Trenitalia (☎ 89201 from a land line or 12 892021 from a mobile; www.trenitalia.it) is partially privatised and runs most of the network. The longest trip is from Ólbia to Cágliari. Some trains run on narrow-gauge track, and many tourists like to take the *trenino verde* (little green train) through some of the most scenic parts of the island. The *trenino verde* only runs in summer (☎ 070 5793 0346; www.treninoverde.com).

 Ferries Local ferries (car and passenger) run regularly from Palau to La Maddalena off the northeast coast. In the southwest there are regular sailings (up to 15 a day) from Portovesme to the Ísola di San Pietro (Carloforte). There are also regular ferries between Santa Teresa di Gallura and Bonifacio on Corsica. Most of the seaside resorts have boat excursions along the coast and islands, including Ísola Tavolara from Porto San Paolo near Ólbia, and the idyllic beaches in the Golfo di Orosei, accessible from Cala Gonone.

 Urban Transport In Cágliari the CTM bus service covers the city and outlying areas. Tickets are valid for 90 minutes (€1) from the first journey, and daily and weekly passes are also available. Tickets can be bought from the kiosk in Piazza Matteotti, in news kiosks and on board. Bus 10 is the most useful line, running from Viale Trento past Corso Vittorio Emanuele to Piazza Garibaldi. No 7 goes from Piazza Matteotti to Castello.

CAR RENTAL

 You must be over 21 and have a full, valid driver's licence and, if not a member of the EU, an international driving permit. Contact your insurance company before departure to check if you are covered outside your home country. It is compulsory to carry all your documents with you while driving.

TAXIS

 Taxis are inexpensive. It's not usually possible to hail them in the street, but there are cab ranks in the larger towns and villages, and your hotel can also book taxis for you. Meters should determine the fare; otherwise, agree a price in advance.

CONCESSIONS

Students/Youths An International Student Identity Card entitles holders to discounts (usually half the normal fee) to museums and archaeological sites. There are three *ostelli per la gioventù* (youth hostels) on the island, which offer cheap accommodation (see www.ostellionline.org).

Senior Citizens Admission to some sites is reduced for those aged 65 (sometimes 60) or over. Note that there are very few facilities for less mobile visitors; only the national museums in Cágliari have wheelchair access.

DRIVING

 Speed limit on main highways: **100kph**. It is Italian law to use your headlights at all times (inlcuding daytime).

 Speed limit on secondary roads: **90kph**

 Speed limit in built-up areas: **50kph**

 Seat belts are compulsory in front seats, and in back seats where fitted. On-the-spot fines are payable by anyone found breaking the law.

 The blood alcohol limit is 0.05%. Random breath tests are carried out. Never drive under the influence of alcohol.

 Petrol is *benzina*, unleaded is *senza piombo*, diesel is *gasolio*. Fuel stations are spaced at regular intervals along SS roads, but most close over lunch and after 7.30pm. However, many are self-service, which take credit cards and euro notes (which must not be dog-eared).

 If your car breaks down, switch on the hazard warning lights and place the red warning triangle (supplied with all rental cars) about 50m behind your vehicle and call the emergency breakdown number (☎ 116). If you are involved in an accident, put out the red warning triangle and call the police (☎ 112/113).

PHOTOGRAPHY

 Photography is forbidden: near military installations, in some churches and monasteries with flash. **Film and digital:** films are not always so easy to find due to the widespread use of digital cameras. While camera shops stock the most popular speeds, if you want to use slides or a fast film, it is better to stock up in advance. Shops in the cities now offer a service for burning memory cards onto CD.

PERSONAL SAFETY

You're very unlikely to come across any bandits and Sardinia is one of Italy's safest regions. However, in cities such as Cágliari it makes sense to take the usual precautions, as petty theft related with drug addiction is on the increase.

● Close bags and wear them in front, slung across your body.
● Leave valuables and jewellery in the hotel safe.
● Never leave luggage or other possessions in parked cars.
● Wear your camera and don't leave it unattended in cafés and restaurants.
● Avoid parks late at night.

Police assistance:
☎ **112 or 113**
from any call box

TELEPHONES

Telecom Italia (TI) payphones are on streets and in bars and some restaurants. Usually you need a phone card (*scheda teléfonica*), available in 2, 3, 5 or 10 denominations from newsstands. Tear the perforated corner off before use. Phone tariffs are very expensive, among the highest in Europe. To get through to an English-speaking operator, dial 170; for directory enquiries in Italy dial 1254.

International Dialling Codes	
From Sardinia to:	
UK:	00 44
USA:	00 1
Germany:	00 49
Spain:	00 34

POST

The postal service is very slow. You can buy stamps (*francobolli*) at the post office (*ufficio postale*), designated by a yellow sign (🅟 Mon–Sat 8–1 and in bigger towns 4–6). If your letter is urgent, send it by the express service *posta prioritaria*. Stamps are also available at tobacconists (*tabacchi*), designated by a big 'T', usually black on white.

HEALTH

 Insurance
EU citizens can reclaim medical expenses if they travel with a European Health Insurance Card (EHIC). These cards are valid for up to five years, and in the UK are available from post offices or online at www.dh.gov.uk. There are also reciprocal arrangements between the Australian Medicare system and Italy, but it is still advisable to take out travel insurance. Ask at a pharmacy or your hotel for details of English-speaking doctors.

 Dental Services
Try to avoid dental treatment if at all possible, as it is not covered by the health service and costs can be exorbitant.

 Sun Advice
Sardinia enjoys long hot summers. The heat is often tempered by cooling breezes, but don't let these fool you into underestimating the strength of the sun. High-factor sun cream, a hat and plenty of water are strongly recommended. Follow the locals' lead and avoid the midday sun.

 Drugs
Prescriptions and other medicines are available from *farmacie* (pharmacies), indicated by a large green cross.

 Safe Water
Tap water is drinkable almost everywhere and especially prized from mountain springs, which you will find in the interior. Bottled water, *acqua minerale*, is also universally available. A sign saying *acqua non potabile* means that the water is unsafe for drinking.

LANGUAGE

The Sardinian language is a melting pot of many influences. Around Alghero you will hear Catalan, for example, which is no surprise, since hundreds of years of Spanish rule have left their mark. However, if there is one language from which *sardo* takes its root, it is Latin; it is much closer to this mother tongue than mainland Italian is. Examples include *domus* (house), which is used in the Sard language in place of the Italian *casa*.

hotel	albergo	with/without	con/senza
room	camera	bath/shower	bagon/doccia
one/two nights	una notte/due notti	with air-conditioning	con aria condizionata
one week	una settimana	with a balcony	con una terrazza
for one/two	per una persona/due	does that include	è includa la prima
people/three people	persone/tre persone	breakfast?	colazione?
with a double bed	con un letto matrimo-niale	camp site	un camping
		youth hostel	ostello per la gioventù

bank	banco	traveller's cheque	assegno di viaggio
exchange office	cambio	do you accept credit	accettate carte di
I want to change	voglio cambiare del	cards?	credito?
money	denaro	how much?	quanto costa?
post office	posta	it's too expensive	è troppo caro
money	denaro	it's cheap	non è caro

I'd like to book a	vorrei prenotare un	water	acqua
table	tavolo	coffee	caffè
do you have a table	avete un tavolo per	milk	latte
for two?	due?	bread	pane
fixed-price menu	menu a prezzo fisso	meat	carne
dish of the day	piatto del giorno	fish	pesce
wine list	lista dei vini	shellfish	crostacei
red/white wine	vino rosso/bianco	vegetables	contorni

aeroplane	aero	bus station	autostazione
airport	aeroporto	railway station	stazione ferroviaria
bus	autobus	ferry terminal	stazione marittima
train	treno	port	porto
car	macchina	ticket	biglietto
car hire	autonoleggi	one way	solo andata
taxi	taxi	return	andata e ritorno
ferry	traghetto	what time does it leave?	a che ora parte?

yes/no	si/non	I'm sorry	mi dispiace
please	per favore/piacere	how are you?	come sta?
thank you	grazie	I'm fine, thank you	bene, grazie
you're welcome	prego/di niente	excuse me	scusi
good morning	buon giorno	I would like	vorrei
good afternoon/	buona sera	open	aperto
evening		closed	chiuso
good night	buona notte	today	oggi
hello/goodbye	ciao (informal)	tomorrow	domani
I don't understand	non capisco	left	sinistra
do you speak English?	parla inglese?	right	destra

REMEMBER

- Confirm your flight the day before departure.

- Arrive 2 hours before your scheduled flight departure time. Ensure that you have all necessary documentation ready. Check on goods allowed in hand luggage.

- Allowances for exporting goods vary with destination – check before departure.

Index

TwinPack
Sardinia

Written by Adele Evans
Verified by Mary McLean
Produced by AA Publishing
Project editor Edith Summerhayes
Copy editor Stephanie Smith
Designer Catherine Murray
Series editor Cathy Hatley

A CIP catalogue record for this book is available from the British Library.

ISBN 978-0-7495-5716-4

The contents of this publication are believed correct at the time of printing. Nevertheless, the publishers cannot be held responsible for any errors or omissions or for changes in the details given in this guide or for the consequences of any reliance on the information provided by the same. This does not affect your statutory rights. Assessments of attractions, hotels, restaurants and so forth are based upon the author's own personal experience and, therefore, descriptions given in this guide necessarily contain an element of subjective opinion which may not reflect the publishers' opinion or dictate a reader's own experiences on another occasion. We have tried to ensure accuracy in this guide, but things do change and we would be grateful if readers would advise us of any inaccuracies they may encounter.

Material in this book may have appeared in other AA publications.

Published by AA Publishing, a trading name of Automobile Association Developments Limited, whose registered office is Fanum House, Basing View, Basingstoke, Hampshire, RG21 4EA. Registered number 1878835.

© **AUTOMOBILE ASSOCIATION DEVELOPMENTS LIMITED 2008**
First published 2008

Colour separation by Keenes, Andover
Printed and bound by Everbest Printing Co. Limited, China

ACKNOWLEDGEMENTS
The Automobile Association would like to thank the following photographers, companies and picture libraries for their assistance in the preparation of this book. Abbreviations for the picture credits are as follows: (t) top; (b) bottom; (c) centre; (l) left; (r) right; (AA) AA World Travel Library.

ALAMY © CuboImages srl/Alamy 24b, 46. EUROPEAN CENTRAL BANK 87.

All the remaining pictures used in this publication are held in the Automobile Association's own photo library (AA World Photo Library) and were taken by Neil Setchfield with the exception of the following which were taken by Clive Sawyer:
1, 6, 23t, 29t, 29b, 30b.

Front cover images: AA/Neil Setchfield; back cover, top to bottom: (a) AA/Neil Setchfield; (b) AA/Neil Setchfield; (c) AA/Neil Setchfield; (d) Photodisc.

Every effort has been made to trace the copyright holders, and we apologise in advance for any accidental errors. We would be happy to apply the corrections in the following edition of this publication.

The author would like to thank Alison, Polly and Hugh from Just Sardinia in England for arranging car hire, assistance with accommodation and their boundless enthusiasm. Many thanks also to Martin for his great support, Renata, the Italian Tourist Board in London, Marina Tavolata from Travel Marketing in Rome, Sally and 'Sir Rupert'.

A03017
Maps in this title produced from mapping © Freytag-Berndt u. Artaria KG, 1231 Vienna-Austria

TITLES IN THE TWINPACK SERIES

Dear **TwinPack** Traveller

Your comments, opinions and recommendations are very important to us. So please help us to improve our travel guides by taking a few minutes to complete this simple questionnaire.

You do not need a stamp (unless posted outside the UK). If you do not want to cut this page from your guide, then photocopy it or write your answers on a plain sheet of paper.

Send to: **The Editor, AA TwinPack Travel Guides, FREEPOST SCE 4598, Basingstoke RG21 4GY.**

Your recommendations…

We always encourage readers' recommendations for restaurants, nightlife or shopping – if your recommendation is used in the next edition of the guide, we will send you a *FREE* **AA TwinPack Guide** of your choice. Please state below the establishment name, location and your reasons for recommending it.

_____

_____

_____

_____

Please send me **AA TwinPack**

Algarve ☐ Andalucía ☐ Corfu ☐ Costa Blanca ☐
Costa Brava ☐ Costa del Sol ☐ Crete ☐ Croatia ☐
Cyprus ☐ Dubai ☐ Gran Canaria ☐ Lanzarote & Fuerteventura ☐
Madeira ☐ Mallorca ☐ Malta & Gozo ☐ Menorca ☐
Provence & the Côte d'Azur ☐ Sardinia ☐ Sicily ☐ Tenerife ☐
(please tick as appropriate)

About this guide…

Which title did you buy?

AA *TwinPack* _____

Where did you buy it? _____

When? m m / y y

Why did you choose an AA *TwinPack* Guide? _____

_____

_____

_____

Did this guide meet your expectations?

Exceeded ☐ Met all ☐ Met most ☐ Fell below ☐

Please give your reasons _____

_____

_____

continued on next page…

Were there any aspects of this guide that you particularly liked? _____

_____

_____

Is there anything we could have done better? _____

_____

_____

About you…

Name *(Mr/Mrs/Ms)* _____

    Address _____

_____

    _____ Postcode _____

    Daytime tel no _____

Please only give us your mobile phone number if you wish to hear from us about other products and services from the AA and partners by text or mms.

Which age group are you in?

    Under 25 ❑   25–34 ❑   35–44 ❑   45–54 ❑   55–64 ❑   65+ ❑

How many trips do you make a year?

    None ❑   One ❑   Two ❑   Three or more ❑

Are you an AA member? Yes ❑   No ❑

About your trip…

When did you book? m m / y y   When did you travel? m m / y y

How long did you stay? _____

Was it for business or leisure? _____

Did you buy any other travel guides for your trip?

    If yes, which ones? _____

Thank you for taking the time to complete this questionnaire. Please send it to us as soon as possible, and remember, you do not need a stamp *(unless posted outside the UK)*.

Happy Holidays!